"Finally, fellow spectrumite Michael McManmon has put his personal and professional success on paper. Having known Michael for almost a decade, it was a prior shame not to have the founder of the trailblazing College Internship Program share his 'recipes' with others. A must-read for the parents of emerging young adults on the spectrum."

—*Michael John Carley, Executive Director of GRASP (The Global and Regional Asperger Syndrome Partnership) and ASTEP (Asperger Syndrome Training and Employment Partnership), and author of* Asperger's From the Inside Out, *USA*

"Michael McManmon's book makes an outstanding contribution to the support, development, and happiness of people on the autism spectrum. It is written with the parents of people with Asperger's Syndrome in mind to help them understand how they can best help their children into adulthood. This book should certainly be studied by professionals employed in the field. The ideas are, above all, practical and based upon experience. They do not depend upon expensive technology but on common-sense based upon observations and sympathetic understanding of the problem. It is written with that detail, insight, and honesty which is only gifted to those with at least one foot in the spectrum."

—*Paul Shattock, Chairman of ESPA and President of the World Autism Organisation, UK*

"*Made for Good Purpose* has a powerful set of tools based on Dr. Michael McManmon's personal experiences and insights as a self-advocate of Asperger's Syndrome. Dr. McManmon defines 'The Donkey Rule,' which will be embraced by every reader, as he guides everyone on a path towards achieving their fullest potential."

—*Lawrence P. Kaplan, Ph.D., Chairman of US Autism & Asperger Association, and author of* Diagnosis Autism: Now What?

"For all the young people who come through our high schools, we must be their guides toward self-knowledge, self-advocacy, and self-determination. In order to do that well, we need the very best guides ourselves. Dr. McManmon is one of those guides, and this book gives us many tools and stories to inform our work."

—*Michael G. McDonald, special educator, San Anselmo, California, USA of related interest*

Developing College Skills in Students with Autism and Asperger's Syndrome
Sarita Freedman
Foreword by Tony Attwood
ISBN 978 1 84310 917 4

Top Tips for Asperger Students
How to Get the Most Out of University and College
Rosemary Martin
Illustrated by Caitlin Cooper
ISBN 978 1 84905 140 8

Guiding Your Teenager with Special Needs through the Transition from School to Adult Life
Tools for Parents
Mary Korpi
ISBN 978 1 84310 874 0

The Social and Life Skills MeNu
A Skill Building Workbook for Adolescents with Autism Spectrum Disorders
Karra M. Barber
ISBN 978 1 84905 861 2

60 Social Situations and Discussion Starters to Help Teens on the Autism Spectrum Deal with Friendships, Feelings, Conflict and More
Seeing the Big Picture
Lisa A. Timms
ISBN 978 1 84905 862 9

Made for Good Purpose

What Every Parent Needs to Know to Help Their Adolescent with Asperger's, High Functioning Autism or a Learning Difference Become an Independent Adult

Michael P. McManmon, Ed.D.
Foreword by Stephen M. Shore, Ed.D.

Jessica Kingsley *Publishers*
London and Philadelphia

First published in 2012
by Jessica Kingsley Publishers
116 Pentonville Road
London N1 9JB, UK
and
400 Market Street, Suite 400
Philadelphia, PA 19106, USA

www.jkp.com

Copyright © Michael P. McManmon 2012
Foreword copyright © Stephen M. Shore 2012
Illustrations copyright © Michael P. McManmon 2012

Library of Congress Cataloging in Publication Data
McManmon, Michael P.
  Made for good purpose : what every parent needs to know to help their adolescent
with Asperger's, high functioning autism, or a learning difference, become an
independent adult / Michael P. McManmon ; foreword by Stephen Shore.
    p. cm.
  Includes bibliographical references and index.
  ISBN 978-1-84905-863-6 (alk. paper)
  1. Asperger's syndrome in adolescence. 2. Learning disabilities--Treatment. I. Title.
RJ506.A9M44 2012
616.85'883200835--dc23
                            2011046529

British Library Cataloguing in Publication Data
A CIP catalogue record for this book is available from the British Library

ISBN 978 1 84905 863 6
eISBN 978 0 85700 435 2

Printed and bound in the United States

I dedicate this book to "all the parents who have young adults on the Asperger's, autism, and learning differences spectrum." You are the ones "fighting the good fight" each and every day. You are turning over every rock, stone, and pebble to find help, guidance, and advice for your sons and daughters. You are the driving force behind my work and your children are my inspiration.

Thank you for your unconditional trust during the past 28 years that the College Internship Program (CIP) has been in existence. With the publication of this book, I continue to push forward the agenda for helping and motivating your sons and daughters. Your determination in pursuing every resource possible to find answers and solutions for your adolescents gives full meaning and purpose to my life's work.

Thank you for everything, especially your encouragement.

Michael P. McManmon

A Word of Thanks

To all of my students and staff (past and present) for your hard work and dedication. To Francine Britton for believing in my voice and your vision. To my children for seeing through my "Aspie" traits and being patient, kind, and loving to me. To Tracy for all your love and continued support. To my mom who always believed in her "Aspie" son. To my dad for all his hard work and for the many fine examples of unselfishness that he gave to me throughout my lifetime.

Contents

Foreword

Michael, my "Aspie cousin," is about to take you on a journey like no other. He's going to tell you a story of the power of positive self-regard and awareness combined with implementing one's strengths to lead a fulfilling and productive life. The unique aspect is that, in the process, Michael has become a leader in helping others with autism and related conditions do the same.

Almost a decade ago I received an invitation to visit a center for college-aged individuals in Lee, Massachusetts, that focused on helping people with Asperger's Syndrome and related conditions achieve success in higher education and employment. A badly needed service, I thought, so I went, discussed my own experiences of being on the autism spectrum, and went home. Shortly thereafter, I was asked to sit on the advisory board of the College Internship Program (CIP), which is dedicated to helping young people with autism and related conditions achieve success both academically and in work.

You are now holding a powerful set of tools based on Michael's personal experiences and insights of having Asperger's Syndrome, hours of hard work put in by collaborators, board members, and staff, and stories from hundreds of individuals benefitting from their involvement in CIP and achieving success *with the strengths of,* rather than *in spite of,* having Asperger's Syndrome.

Where does success begin? It starts with knowing oneself—strengths, challenges, and everything in between. Launching from an initial unofficial diagnosis from his co-workers, we see how Michael turns his Aspie powers of focusing on a special interest or passion to develop greater understanding of what having Asperger's Syndrome means to him—and the beginnings of the reframing process of what it means to have Asperger's Syndrome or a related condition for individuals attending CIP.

Employing personal experiences and those of others with Asperger's Syndrome, we learn how the author uses his hard-won realizations towards being the best Michael he can be—with Asperger's Syndrome. One area explored is the parent–child relationship, where the time and effort parents and others supporting people on the autism spectrum expend tends to be more intensive than raising a typical child. Additionally, the supporting adult is commonly the only reliable interpreter of the confusing, unpredictable outside world, leading often to a very tight and possibly dependent relationship between that adult and the child with autism.

As a result, successful navigation through the developmentally appropriate separation of the child from their parents or significant caretakers often becomes even more challenging than it usually is for the typical individual. This book examines how to transform that "steel umbilical cord" between parents and their almost adult child into a successful two-way relational road based on mutual respect. This was knowledge that would have been very helpful during the early days of my marriage of more than two decades.

Michael's insight in developing a personal "board of advisors" of individuals who can be trusted to be called upon for advice is one of many a gemstone-cutting tool described in this book. Whether being on the autism spectrum or not, it continues to help Michael, me, and countless others to have people who can reliably tell us when we are really seeing a donkey and not a horse, so as to avoid becoming, as so eloquently stated, "a jack***."

True to the name of the organization, much emphasis is placed on achieving success in higher education and employment. For example, the book is chock-full of examples of executive functioning strategies for obtaining and maintaining self-awareness and self-regulation in order to meet the organizational, scheduling, and socialization demands of doing well in college and keeping a job. For example, the seemingly simple yet powerful rule of being on time for morning activities, "once I get up I don't lay back down," is just a great way of starting the day and keeping to one's schedule.

Challenges in social interaction are often the biggest barrier between a person with Asperger's Syndrome and success. The reader will find many examples, tips, and mnemonics to help in teaching social interaction skills. However, as so aptly pointed out and so true to many on the autism spectrum, memorizing the rules of politeness from Emily Post's writing on good manners and Dale Carnegie's work on finding and maintaining friendships does not necessarily mean we know how to put them into practice in real time, and this suggests the need for practice.

In this book the reader will find multiple suggestions for practicing social interaction, from analyzing short video clips of sitcoms for decoding non-verbal communication to spending time with a mentor learning how to interact successfully in real-world situations such as with a cashier in a supermarket, with classmates in school, or co-workers on a job site.

I have just described a small number of the tools Michael's experiences and CIP bring forth for people with Asperger's Syndrome. Readers will find that, while this book focuses on achieving success for people on the autism spectrum, many of the realizations, insights, and suggestions will be helpful to all.

In summary, it has been a pleasure and honor to observe Michael and CIP successfully grow to where both are making positive contributions to the lives of an increasing number of people with Asperger's Syndrome and related conditions. I look forward to the future as Michael and CIP continue on their path of successfully preparing young adults be the best they can be, not *in spite of* having, but rather *because* they have, Asperger's Syndrome.

When you have finished reading this powerful tool kit, you will see exactly how the "poster boy of adult Asperger's Syndrome diagnosis" has successfully employed his journey of personal and professional growth in the education and leadership of all on the autism spectrum who desire greater fulfillment in a life dedicated to good purpose—and what it means to be human.

Stephen M. Shore, Ed.D.

Opening Statement

Michael as a small child

You and I have come a long way since we were young, unknowing, and full of innocence. We have survived deserts of fear and climbed mountains of strength. We have experienced the joys and heartbreaks of building or letting go of relationships. Together, we have emerged (albeit) slowly to a safe place and learned to speak our truth: out loud; now knowing the joy of being ourselves.

Introduction

Show me imperfection and I'll show you love: setting the brilliant course of caring and acceptance.

After graduating from college, I rented an inexpensive studio apartment in Emmitsburg, Maryland. I sat down on the floor among my few possessions and stared at the wall. When it got dark, I curled up in a sleeping bag and slept. I stayed there for the better part of three days doing absolutely nothing, bewildered about how to take the next steps in my life. I had no idea how to become a valuable, functional, independent adult. I knew I had an intelligent mind, but I also knew that in key areas I was a misfit. I was naïve, always misreading social situations and acting in a way that I now know was immature. This was due (I now realize) to my Asperger's Syndrome, a form of autism, although it would be many years before I would receive a diagnosis.[1]

Those three days staring at the wall determined my life's work: the genesis of this book. I am the founder of the College Internship Program (CIP), a program designed to help young people with Asperger's Syndrome, high-functioning autism, and learning differences make successful transitions from adolescence to young adulthood. CIP gives young adults the tools to become productive members of society, not individuals who end up staring at the wall as I did with no idea how to get started.

The struggle for independence is extremely difficult for young adults on the autism spectrum. They are connected to their parents with what I call "the steel umbilical," a cord that is difficult and painful to cut. The years between 18 and 25 are perilous for young adults with learning differences. It is when the last vestiges of confidence and self-worth are shattered. Instead of transitioning from dependence to independence, parents see their children withdraw. Familiar feelings of anxiety, depression, and a sense of failure or inadequacy intensify.

Parents are frightened about what the future holds for their children. They are unsure of what to do or how to help. They wonder if their son or daughter will ever be able to start or finish college, get or keep a job, or begin and maintain a relationship.

---

1   Hans Asperger (January 18, 1906–October 21, 1980) was the Austrian pediatrician after whom Asperger's Syndrome is named. Asperger's Syndrome was first defined in 1944.

As loving parents, they see sensitive and intelligent people, trapped by anger and resentment, who are inflexible, blaming others for their difficulties and disappointments. They watch as their adolescents isolate and withdraw deeper and deeper into a shell of low self-esteem and heartbreaking insecurity.

Professionals who work with young people on the autism spectrum are also at a loss. High schools and colleges are trying to cope with large numbers of students who have Asperger's Syndrome. For the past 20 or 30 years, schools have managed to deal successfully with learning differences by providing standardized accommodations and support systems. However, the services needed for students diagnosed with Asperger's Syndrome are limited or non-existent. This vulnerable population faces overwhelming challenges as they move from adolescence to young adulthood and their parents are left to pick up the pieces when their sons and daughters (through no fault of their own) fall apart.

I've learned, not only from my professional work at CIP's six centers during the past 28 years (and from ten years of operating group homes for youngsters with learning differences and emotional difficulties) but also from my own life experiences, that true self-knowledge is the key to empowering young adults with Asperger's, autism, or learning differences. Enabling these young men and women to deal productively with the challenges they face helps them to release the sense of failure and despair that has plagued them for most of their lives. Self-knowledge about their differences is the first step to achieving self-acceptance. It is the foundation for developing the unique and considerable talents and gifts each one possesses and then teaching them how to function "in" and contribute "to" society using these attributes.

Made for Good Purpose imparts the insights and strategies I have developed over the many years that I have spent working with hundreds and hundreds of young people. Helping them master basic social, academic, and life skills leading to success in college or career training, and then preparing them to start working in the world and living independently, has been a privilege. The following chapters contain parts of my own story, the stories of former students and their families, as well as practical "how to" advice for helping parents and their (soon to be adult) children move forward.

There is a tremendous need for the kind of support CIP or a CIP-"type" program provides, but it is staff intensive and expensive. This cost, unfortunately, puts it out of the reach of many families. We have developed a non-profit to assist with tuition. Many parents are not aware that programs like CIP exist. While CIP's outreach efforts are extensive, this program and others like it are not nearly enough to reach the increasing number of young people diagnosed with Asperger's Syndrome or learning differences.

The need to help this growing at-risk population is enormous. It is my hope that this book will raise awareness about the challenges young adults on the autism spectrum face. *Made for Good Purpose* is a tool kit for parents. The underlying theme of this book and the heart of the work we do every single day is that "you were made for good purpose and are inherently valuable." This book offers support and guidance to parents so that they can help their sons and daughters grow into strong, confident, engaged adults.

Made for Good Purpose offers practical advice, based on theory and research, that will help your son or daughter master the basics needed in order to live independently. It also shows you how to help your young adult obtain the skills necessary for life and work or for college and career training.

Chapter 1

Understanding Your Diagnosis

The Power of Knowing

I was in my own mind, keeping my eyes averted; reading, staring into space. What was I thinking? What were my hopes and dreams?

The diagnosis of Asperger's, autism, or a learning difference sets the stage for your son or daughter to obtain the self-awareness and self-confidence necessary to make a successful transition from adolescence to adulthood.

Receiving a diagnosis is only a beginning. Most CIP students are at least 18 years old when they enter the program. However, as their parents will attest, they have little self-understanding of their diagnosis. They do not know what their individual profile of strengths and challenges looks like. These young men and women do not know how to go about becoming self-sufficient, independent, and productive adults. They are often unaware of the unique, positive attributes they bring to the world.

I know from experience that young people with Asperger's, autism, or a learning difference usually run from this diagnosis. As Mark Twain said: "Denial ain't just a river in Egypt." They feel threatened and defensive; they do not want to be different (the anathema of adolescence). They think, "If I don't fit in, then I don't belong. I'm not going to deal with this; it's too painful and scary!"

When these young adults look at their friends and peers, they convince themselves (in spite of an official diagnosis) that everyone has minor differences and that they are no different from anyone else. They think in broad strokes about what it means to have a disability, and conclude that it does not apply to them. These young people want to blend in, and no parent or teacher can blame them for this. They are smart in limited areas, but they think they are smart across the board, even though they have obvious, debilitating blind spots.

I know about this from my own life. It was not until after my diagnosis in my 50s that I recognized my social deficits and began to try to accept them. When I speak at conferences and seminars, I always say, "I am the poster-boy for late diagnosis." So much changed since that fateful day in 2003, when CIP's Academic Dean, Marjorie, walked into my office and asked if she could talk to me. She started by saying: "Michael, I don't want to upset you, or offend you or make you angry, but I have something important to say to you and I hope you will hear me out." She was reluctant and a little nervous. Before beginning, Marjorie talked a lot about "having my best interests at heart."

Of course, I wondered whom I had offended, or what I had said that was inappropriate. I felt like I was about to get one of those "lectures" my staff give me from time to time when they are trying to set me straight. So I tried as hard as I could to "listen and not judge" what she was about to say.

Marjorie tentatively unfolded the pieces of paper she had in her hand and said, "This is a list of the characteristics of individuals with Asperger's Syndrome." She went on to say that, after talking it over with several other staff members, they felt that I had most of these traits. She then gave examples of situations and incidents that had occurred during the past ten years. She pointed out that my behavior exhibited the characteristics of a person diagnosed with Asperger's Syndrome.

Before she got very far down the list, I told her that I had been thinking about this too, and for quite some time. I told her about the rigidity of my thought processes, my problems making eye contact, and my trouble with relationships, to name a few things.

My late-in-life diagnosis explains many of the situations and difficulties I experienced as a child and that I was continuing to experience as an adult. I was the sleepy child whose desk was put in front of the blackboard for half the year in second grade—not because I was disruptive, but because I could not stop doing what I considered my special interest: drawing war ships and airplanes!

Marjorie was kind, caring, and compassionate. By taking a chance and having this "talk" with me, she helped me get to the point where I could look at my past and present behavior. As an adult with Asperger's, I needed to get past denial and resistance and start taking my own journey toward self-acceptance, self-awareness, and self-advocacy. I knew that I needed to start practicing what I had been teaching others, and begin to use my diagnosis as a source of strength. Shortly after my diagnosis, I met Dr. Stephen Shore, whom I call my "Aspie cousin." Stephen became a supportive role model for me. As I read his first book, *Beyond the Wall* (2003),

I focused on the section where he talks about training himself to identify non-verbal cues. I read this section and then reread it until I was able to practice and start applying the techniques he described. I focused on improving my reciprocal conversation skills. Stephen's book, his practical advice, and his techniques for integrating this advice into daily life helped me become more astute. Through his friendship, Stephen helped me recognize my assets and strengths (including my perseverance and loyalty) and encouraged me to "just go for it!"

For example, at the time I was reading Stephen's book, I was flying back and forth between Melbourne, Florida, and Lee, Massachusetts, developing a new program (The Brevard Center). Every day I would call my girlfriend and tell her all the things I was doing. I would go on and on and on! I did this a couple of times daily, figuring that I was appropriately maintaining my relationship with her.

However, when I returned home, my senses would be so overloaded from the flight, the drive, and the long day that I would come into our house, give her a kiss, sit down, and turn on the TV. She would come over and sit by me, turn the TV off, take my hands, look me in the eyes, and have a "feedback session."

Before my diagnosis, I would have tuned her out. I would have been unresponsive, vacantly nodding my head, my attention focused elsewhere. However, after my diagnosis and some serious self-awareness, I made a conscious effort to engage in conversation with her.

The next time I went to Florida, I called her every day. I told her "some" but "not all" of what I was doing and then asked, "How was your day?" Then came the worst part—I had to listen to her answer for what seemed like an eternity (it was only a minute or two). Then, feeling buoyed by my newfound ability, I asked an even tougher question: "How do you feel?"

Over time and with practice I learned to prepare myself for re-entry. The next time, after the long flight, I came into the house, sat down, took her hand, looked in her eyes, gave her a kiss, told her that I'd missed her, and asked how she was—and listened. Then, ten minutes later, I turned on the TV! For someone with Asperger's Syndrome this was enormous progress and my self-esteem soared. I often tell this story to young adults to illustrate how receiving a diagnosis gave me a road map to follow and helped me improve my social and emotional understanding and, in turn, my well-being.

Months after my diagnosis, Marjorie returned to my office, this time bearing a book entitled *Thinking in Pictures* (1995) by Dr. Temple Grandin. She said, "Michael, you need to read this book. It describes you." I looked at the book, saw that it had a cow on the front cover, and was puzzled. She said, "Just force yourself to get through the chapters until you get to the final two, even though you may be bored with all the talk about cattle." She was extremely insistent and I agreed to read it. I did have to force myself to read minutia regarding cattle processes for what seemed like an eternity until I finally reached the last two chapters. Then I simply could not put the book down. I was transfixed. Finally, someone was describing the way "I" think. I have always been a visual thinker and learner, possessing an uncanny photographic memory. I was never able to learn by listening to a teacher talk or lecture in front of a class. I finished Temple's book understanding more and more about myself, feeling like I had just read my own personal *Declaration of Independence.* Who would have ever thought (certainly not me, at that point) that eight years later I would be sharing a stage with Temple Grandin at professional conferences, telling my own story to others and talking about my own "thinking in pictures" experiences.

The most crucial step parents can take to help young adults understand their diagnosis is to explain to them that the particular pattern of assets and challenges they have is called Asperger's Syndrome. Discovering that there is a name for "what" they have, and a set of criteria that matches "who" they are and "how" they act, can help free those on the autism spectrum from self-blame.

In my case, the diagnostic label that I would assign to others and that now applied to me was presented in a constructive, caring way. Marjorie helped me understand my difficulties and I began preparing a plan of self-instruction, asking for help and acquiring skills for my most challenging problems—including my social understanding difficulties.

The reality and truth for me at this later stage of life was that my diagnosis was an enormous relief. I could finally put a name to my way of being in the world and start understanding the impact that Asperger's has had on my life and work. I know that without my diagnosis I would have gone on with my cognitive rigidity unchecked for the rest of my life.

With diagnosis, the journey to self-awareness and self-acceptance begins. The following story about John and Julia illustrates, from two decidedly different angles, how taking this momentous journey toward self-acceptance, albeit by different and unique routes, played out in both their lives. The story, compiled by CIP staff and adapted for this chapter, is an excellent example of the "power" that accepting a diagnosis brings.

JOHN AND JULIA

John enrolled at our Berkshire Center in Massachusetts in September 1999. Prior to enrollment, he had completed three semesters at a local community college near his home but was unable to connect socially with other students. Difficulties with time and personal management led to frustration and failure. John decided to take some time off. He knew he needed a supportive setting in order to experience success but was resistant. John's decision to enroll in CIP's program the following year was made with a lot of input from his parents and was timely and appropriate.

When John arrived for orientation, my staff knew that he was more familiar with frustration than with success. Born prematurely and with medical problems in a poor, rural area in Central America, John's infancy was unstable. Adoption by a young couple from the United States, followed by subsequent surgical operations, gave him his health and a second chance. His adoptive parents provided a lot of love and security, but they moved almost every year during his childhood. As a result, John was not able to make long-lasting friendships during his formative years. His learning disabilities were diagnosed in the third grade, and made him feel even more isolated and frustrated. John learned to seek refuge by developing and living in a fantasy world.

Emerging at this young age were depression, anger, shame, guilt, and a feeling of victimization. John received an official diagnosis of depression and Attention Deficit Hyperactive Disorder (ADHD). Some signs of Asperger's Syndrome, such as rigid thinking, social cue problems, and poor eye contact, were noted. He entered into therapy and began to feel and do better. When his family moved, after being in one place for five years, John had to start over once again for his last two years of high school—a real setback.

The frustration and isolation John experienced in high school intensified when he entered community college. He wanted to be independent, but living in an apartment alone and without a support system did not work out for him. He needed more structure and self-awareness to experience success.

Before entering CIP at age 22, John had received a further diagnosis of Asperger's Syndrome from the Yale Child Study Center. The study also noted deep-seated depression, social anxiety, and significant, unfulfilled cravings for relationships, as well as serious deficits in adaptive functioning. John suffered from low self-esteem and a severely limited sense of responsibility. He had very little insight into the role he played in the "reactions" of other people to him.

At CIP John acknowledged his Asperger's diagnosis, but could not accept its implications or its possibilities. He used CIP's therapy and support systems for comfort, and for dealing with everyday problems and the difficulties of a limited social life. He made progress in some important areas of his life, but the mention of Asperger's was met with shame and resistance. He attended several on-campus modules to deal with this resistance, but he tended to put his head down and sleep through them. He just was not ready. He relied on his vivid fantasy life to escape from feelings of frustration and failure. He blamed others for his misfortunes and did not understand that his own power and resourcefulness could make things better.

When John started his second year in our program, he
met Julia. She was a brand-new, first-year student at CIP. Her
diagnosis was also Asperger's Syndrome. Julia received her
official diagnosis at the age of eight. Her parents began working
with her daily in areas of self-acceptance and self-esteem. Julia
learned about her diagnosis and that it was called Asperger's
Syndrome at this early age. She also connected with a therapist
who taught her coping skills. Strong-willed Julia achieved
hard-earned successes with the help of dedicated teachers. Her
parents also realized that, in order for their daughter to have
continued success when she entered college, a strong support
program would be necessary. Julia and her parents visited several
programs and decided on a full-time residential program at CIP.

The big difference between John and Julia was that she
accepted her diagnosis. As luck would have it, Julia befriended
John during her first week at CIP. As they got to know each
other during her first few weeks on campus, John soon noticed
that Julia (now that she was away from her parents and her
sheltered high school setting) was willing to work hard to learn
as much as she could about coping with her diagnosis. She then
worked even harder to implement all that she was learning at
CIP. John saw how determined she was to succeed in spite of
her Asperger's Syndrome. In time, as their friendship grew, Julia
became a terrific role model for John.

When Julia and John started dating, John began to slowly
change his thought processes. He was less angry about
his diagnosis and more open to talking to staff, his peers, his
family, and others about how his Asperger's was affecting
his day-to-day life on campus, at his college, and in establishing
a relationship with Julia.

This was a real turning point for John. He finally had the
girlfriend he had always dreamed of and a fellow "Aspie" to relate
to for the first time in his life. As for Julia, she was determined
to do well for herself and was happy to bring John along with
her. John could not resist. With Julia's strong influence over him,
and the structure and support of CIP's program and staff, John
flourished for the rest of the year. When he left the program at
the end of 2000, he returned home with coping skills, support

systems, true self-knowledge, and acceptance of his Asperger's Syndrome diagnosis.

John is now working regularly and functioning at a responsible level. Julia and John are still good friends and both are currently dating other people while emailing and texting each other frequently. John continues on his personal journey toward even greater acceptance and independence while Julia went on to a four-year college after no longer needing a support program. John needed the kind and loving care that a true friend provided, as well as the skills for life and work he obtained from a structured, supportive program. The most important factor, acceptance of a diagnosis, allowed John to get to the point where he is now and allowed Julia to achieve total independence.

Julia did for John what Marjorie did for me (minus the romantic attachment of course) by offering understanding and non-judgmental, unconditional support. Julia transferred to the four-year college after spending two years in CIP's program. She lives independently, works full time, and continues to do exceptionally well.

When confronted with peers who have the same diagnosis and who model self-acceptance and success, your son or daughter will begin to succeed too. John found immense relief in talking to Julia and, eventually, to other friends and staff, especially his social mentor at CIP. While Julia's friendship was the initial motivator, once John accepted his Asperger's diagnosis he got involved in his own life by connecting with others, absorbing and learning techniques for social interaction, and mastering self-care routines. By attending CIP classes and individual sessions, and not sleeping through them, John became empowered and was able to achieve his own successes in life.

"I am an Apple"

During the early days at CIP, I searched for an analogy to help students accept and understand their individual diagnosis. I came up with "I am an Apple computer in a PC world." Most people use PC computers. They are easy to operate and predictable. Apple computers process differently. They do graphics, visual design, music, and all the things that regular PCs cannot do. Objectively, you would not say an Apple computer is disabled or defective because it does things differently from a PC.

In the Asperger's, autism, and learning differences world, it is as if the PC speaks English and the Apple speaks a foreign language. It is necessary, of course, to learn English to get along in the neurotypical world. This example or interface is often referred to as the social interface, the learning of social competencies. At CIP we teach young adults that, as Apple computers operating in a PC world, they have distinct and unique advantages and that it is "OK" to access the world in a different way. Students "can" and "do" learn how to successfully integrate into the PC world and still maintain their Apple identity.

I know that our students have areas of superior performance in which they outshine all their peer groups. Even though they tend to look at their diagnosis as a deficit, my staff and I help them see that they are actually more competent than others in many areas and that they are simply in an "Apple" minority. We help them understand that it is incumbent and important for them to fit into the neurotypical world, not the other way around.

If young adults are serious about getting on with their lives and learning skills for life and work, we will help them. Once they understand that the key to changing their perception of their diagnosis means putting equal time and energy into learning about non-verbal language and social competencies as they do for their special interests, things start changing in a positive way. The young people start coexisting with comfort in the surrounding PC world.

Our students tend to embrace their "authentic self" naturally. No matter how "therapized" (my word for years and years of psychological help) they are when they come to us, and in spite of the teachers or peers who said they were stupid or bullied them, these young people are still firmly who they were meant to be. This is a plus in our program. Knowing that they can be authentic allows for progress. Once students begin to see that the same goofy characteristics that they ran from in high school and thought were silly are now a source of strength and ability, progress happens rapidly.

I have a saying over my desk that I encourage all students to embrace: "The genuine evokes the genuine." As I impart this knowledge to our students, I also tell them about a daily affirmation that has also worked for me: "When I love and accept me, others will like me too. Wow! How did that happen?"

I know that our students must be courageously honest and willing to learn flexibility. At CIP, young adults find out that doing the same thing repeatedly will bring the same result over and over again. Willingness to change is a core concept all young adults on the autism spectrum will need to master in order to function well and function independently.

In the introduction to this book, I stated, "You were made for good purpose and are inherently valuable." This statement has remained the guiding light at all CIP centers. We also teach parents and their children that Asperger's Syndrome and autism are learning *differences*, not learning *disabilities*. This is not semantics but a real understanding that is necessary to help adolescents and young adults understand and accept who they are.

Diagnosis that leads to true self-understanding opens our students "up" to their new lives. Over the years, I have learned about all the assets behind my differences. Now, as a fully awake adult, I use these assets for good purpose. I can live intentionally, create wonderful things in my life, and be genuinely myself. This is what I want for all young adults with learning differences. My work, during the past quarter of a century, has allowed me the amazing opportunity and privilege of watching hundreds of students "come out" into their own realities.

Once young adults start to accept that they are wonderful the way they are, they grow without fear and learn to self-actualize. Teaching that self-esteem and self-confidence arise naturally when young adults are unafraid to move forward and try new ways of being leads to understanding of why this is so important to master through instruction, practice, and observation. As students become cognitively flexible, start trying new things, and entertain others' ideas, they recognize their own validity. They learn to connect with others and be part of a team. They form alliances, learn to negotiate. They begin to compromise and, most surprisingly, they even start to enjoy and anticipate change.

Being such a visual person and learner, I made a t-shirt one day to proclaim "Change Is My Ally." I wear this one—a lot! It is a visual reminder for me that things are always changing, that progress is being made, and that this is a "good and positive thing."

During a "Person-centered planning" meeting (this is where our students get to state clearly what they think their needs and wants are) at our Berkeley Center in California, a student commented to his parents that he had made some recent changes in his life. He said to them that everyone has bad things happen to them and that sometimes "S _ _ _ Happens." Looking at this a little differently, I sent him a t-shirt a couple of weeks later that said "Shift Happens." This phrase also "took off" and is a popular slogan appearing on t-shirts at all CIP campuses. Seeing students and staff wearing one of these t-shirts is always such a visual, affirming, hopeful, and wonderful start to my day.

Young people with Asperger's and learning differences are often unemployed or under-employed because of their lack of social understanding and executive functioning abilities. They lead lives of isolation with or without a college degree. The default setting, after years of education and therapy, often leads to their going deeper into themselves and pushing the world away. Self-knowledge and understanding show young adults that their good purpose is to be the best "Apple" they can be. It also allows a great deal of "shift" to happen.

Chapter 2

Learning the Art of Letting Go
The Steel Umbilical

*Letting go of the past and consciously deciding that love
and compassion should rule. A new beginning built upon
common suffering, forgiving, and a little willingness to
risk and be open to each other.*

THE END OF PEN AND INK

LIFE CHANGES IN A FLASH —
THERE IS NO GOING BACK.

FROM BLACK + WHITE TO COLOR
FROM A SISTER TO A BROTHER.

STEP OUT OF THE BOX,
DARE TO BE DIFFERENT.

TRY NEW THINGS +
SAMPLE THE WORLD.

TOO LITTLE TIME — BUT ALL THAT IS NEEDED
HAVING NOTHING — BUT ALL THAT I WANT

TAKE THE LONG ROAD HOME
STOP AND HAVE COFFEE WITH A FRIEND
LIVE NATURALLY + FOLLOW THE FLOW
GIVE TO OTHERS BUT NURTURE YOURSELF
IT'S ALRIGHT THE WAY IT IS ....
IT'S JUST,
PLAIN ALRIGHT.
11/13/08

I know that parents with young adults on the autism spectrum realize that they have consciously, or even subconsciously, "taken on" a more involved role in their sons and daughters' lives. They have had to advocate endlessly with school officials and teachers. They have also had to assume the role of social workers and activity directors. It is almost as though there is a "steel umbilical cord" connecting parents to their special needs children. At CIP, we help parents cut this cord—a task that is not easy.

From the beginning, the most important thing parents can do is to frame this process positively. Young adults on the autism spectrum need to realize that, although their parents have had more to say about their lives than parents of those not on the spectrum, this involvement has benefitted them. However, after high school, this type of dependency has a negative effect that hinders progress and stifles growth. In CIP's program, my staff and I know that depending too much on a parent for emotional and day-to-day support can be damaging. What seemed to work in junior high and high school now has a detrimental effect and can negatively influence well-being. We understand and know that your son or daughter may have developed a very close relationship with one parent (most often the mother) and that this relationship often feels "symbiotic"—as though the parent and child have the same thoughts or the same mind. In *I'll Miss You Too*, Steffany Bane writes:

> With Mom, our understanding and tolerance for each other's idiosyncrasies in communication grew with efforts on both parts. Freshman year could be described as a push–pull year for us. At one moment, I was pushing my mother away and at another, I was pulling her close again. I felt she was doing the same. I believe this was subconscious and normal on our parts. (Bane Woodacre and Bane 2006, pp.162–163)

The following story about Jeff and his mother is another good example of the symbiosis just described.

JEFF

Jeff, originally from California, enrolled in CIP's Buffalo, New York, Center, when he was 19 years old. Having graduated from a boarding school for students with learning differences, his IQ was in the superior range. He was articulate, well mannered, and easygoing.

During orientation week at CIP, Jeff's mom attended the session where staff take parents through the process of "letting go." They showed Jeff's mom the best and most effective ways for her to communicate with her son, his advisor, and other staff members, so that Jeff could learn to stand on his own two feet and start taking those critical first steps towards independence.

Two weeks later Jeff's advisor, David, discovered that Jeff's mom was calling him from California to get him up in the morning (4 a.m.—her time) and then calling him many times throughout the day to see how he was doing. She would give him instructions and advice (almost hourly) as to what he should be doing and when he should be doing it. Jeff, in turn, was waiting each day for his mom to call and get him up in the morning and for her to tell him when to take his shower, what to wear, what to make and eat for breakfast, when to go to classes, and the list goes on and on. Staff intervened and, with awareness, coaching, and a lot of ongoing support from Jeff's advisor and other staff members, Jeff's mom was able to back off and start letting go one small step at a time. Jeff could then start taking his own steps toward self-reliance.

At CIP, we know it takes time and a conscious effort to change symbiotic relationships. My staff and I know that parents may feel compelled and almost driven to "hold on to" and manage their sons and daughters' lives on a daily basis. Parents certainly understand how vital it is for their young adult to have more autonomy and more self-direction. As was the case with Jeff and his mom, we know how hard it is for a parent to do this. Young people on the autism spectrum cannot just go "cold turkey" from their parents. During these first few weeks on campus, we work closely and patiently with students and parents to help the transition go as smoothly as possible. I can assure you that "the steel umbilical" is cut slowly, one careful cut at a time—with each section in this chapter detailing and dissecting what you and your young adult can expect. Real-life examples of how CIP staff have helped parents do this with success are explained.

This chapter is a "tool kit" for parents as they help their young adults begin the separation process. It is the methodology given to CIP parents to help their sons and daughters transition away from the safe structure they have known for 18 or more years to the independence needed for success in life and work. It has many poignant stories and a lot of practical advice. You might say that this chapter is the "razor-sharp blade" that cuts "the steel umbilical." Taken one step at a time, this chapter is an excellent tool for letting go and doing so in ways that are effective and appropriate for all young adults on the Asperger's, autism, or learning differences spectrum (from now on called "the autism spectrum").

One step at a time...

So how do you break this dependency that your son or daughter has on you? How do you help your young adult build interdependent relationships with others in order to accomplish this goal? Moreover, how do young adults deal with loneliness and isolation at college or at a program like mine? How do you help them deal with the feelings they have about leaving home? The transition between dependence and independence gives your son or daughter an opportunity to create a different kind of relationship with you and the rest of your family, a relationship that will be long-lasting and meaningful.

I know that your primary concern as a parent at this point is that, if your son or daughter does not rely on you anymore, whom does he or she rely on? I cannot stress how important it is to find mentors who are trained, have strong values, and understand learning differences. Young adults with learning differences need people they can rely on for advice when questions about what to do arise. They need to seek social and academic mentors on and off campus, as well as other advocacy services. The school or program chosen should have these options and services available.

The student disabilities office at the college or career center is an excellent place to start. An advisor or mentor can help young people make an appointment. Then, in talking to the people in the disabilities office, students can state what they need and make choices from what the school or support program offers.

This enables your young adult to start learning to self-advocate. By doing this, he or she will learn to trust in his or her ability to make decisions without you. As choices and options are presented, your son or daughter will realize that it is appropriate and "absolutely fine" to ask for advice and decision-making help from his or her mentor, advisor, and others.

Another way of easing the transition during the first few critical weeks your son or daughter is away is to remember, when he or she calls home or emails you, to talk about the activities you are doing and that you are involved in, and say that all is well at home. This is an excellent way to send the message that things are OK and as they should be. It also sends a "signal" that says you are backing off, letting go, and encouraging independence. This is another "two-way" step in cutting "the steel umbilical."

At times, you might feel that your son or daughter is not communicating enough with you but please put this in context too. Leaving home can be just as hard for you as it is for your young adult. Keep in mind that, if your son or daughter is calling or emailing you several times a day, he or she will not form relationships with advisors, mentors, or peers. If you are encouraging this (as Jeff's mom did), please remember that by not cutting "the steel umbilical" you are keeping your young adult from achieving crucial steps toward independence. I know it is hard, but trust me, from years and years of experience I have learned that when you put the football on the floor and walk out of the room the young person will pick it up.

With the right program and guidance from you, your son or daughter will become more and more aware of the decisions he or she is making every day. Your young adult will develop an instinct, know when additional support or advice is needed, and have the ability to ask for it. The following story about a former student named Robert is a good example of achieving independence by taking initiative and asking advisors and mentors "how" to obtain services needed.

ROBERT

Robert came to our Berkeley, California, Center from a situation where his parents were responsible for making most (if not all) of his decisions for him during his high school years. With a lot of guidance, advice, support, and input from CIP's staff, Robert's parents realized the importance of allowing him to become more independent and how crucial it was for them to cut "the steel umbilical" that they had with their son. Staff then empowered Robert to set out, with their help, to get exactly what he needed to become successful during his time at our center.

At CIP, our program helps students address their needs in several different areas and in several different ways. Robert attended a local two-year college and needed tutoring. With coaching from his academic advisor, he was able to ask his school's disabilities office for additional help in math and English. After talking with his advisor, Robert asked for—and participated in—individual therapy and group social thinking to help him address psychological issues and meet his program's social goals.

Robert disliked cooking and did not know how to do simple tasks such as cleaning, laundry, and grocery shopping. He asked for help with this and received instruction in cooking, as well as residential competencies such as apartment cleaning, wardrobe maintenance, and grocery shopping. To help Robert take this new independence one step further, his advisor showed him how to manage his finances effectively. Robert's career counselor helped him fill out paperwork and find an internship program that imparted the value of a strong work ethic into his daily life.

This comprehensive approach was ideal for Robert. His parents' ability to cut "the steel umbilical" and allow their son to focus on achieving independence, with input from others, was vital to his success. Robert learned to use self-advocacy as a driving force to autonomy and independence.

Robert enrolled in an information technology program at a business school and thrived. After this program, he went on to achieve an Associate's degree. Robert is living independently in Seattle, Washington. He is successful doing work that he likes, and is living a fulfilling life.

Like Robert, I know that your son or daughter can learn to rely on and interact with people trained to foster and support independence. For example, a person who has been a positive role model, or someone whose work has been admired, will become an important part of a network of assistance. I always tell students who are tentative at this point that the President has a cabinet and numerous advisors to consult with on decisions. As students, they need to know how to ask for help or guidance from those around them who are qualified to give it.

As your son or daughter progresses through this important stage of parental separation, he or she will continue to realize that you will always be there. And, most importantly, your young adult will know that this is the time and place to seek support systems and develop a self-advocacy plan for the future. A good program will provide learning difference supports such as tutors and note-takers to assist your son or daughter. Accommodations, such as being allowed to have untimed tests, or additional time to take a test, should be available if needed. Counseling services, internship and employment services, medication services, and nutritional services will help your young adult achieve goals both on campus and in specific off-campus programs. These are appropriate services for anyone on the autism spectrum.

Asking for help...

As I mentioned before, students need to learn to cut their end of "the steel umbilical" by seeking assistance from others. Mentors can show your son or daughter how to press for what is needed. This process is called "individuation" and it is vital. It allows your young adult to feel in control of life and capable of making appropriate decisions by having a sense of self-determination.

Your young adult may be fearful of asking a question or answering one because of past mistakes or a fear of not having the right answer. Your support at this stage can give your son or daughter the courage to ask others for help. At CIP, we tell all our students that asking or answering any question that leads you closer to the correct answer makes you smarter in the end. My staff and I use a number of simple examples: for instance, Thomas Edison did not succeed at making the light bulb the first time around. It took him 999 attempts and "tries" before he discovered that the right combination of metals would work (tungsten). He had to ask and find answers for many questions until he could figure out the right combination of materials to make his light bulb work. You could say all those attempts were mistakes or you could reframe your perception and say that he had 999 approximations to the right answer. This same process and procedure applies to most inventions in the modern world. Everything we learn brings us closer to doing things better and having our life work better for us. I often tell students that I have never had a student fail at anything as long as he or she was willing to ask for help and prepared to approach things from a new or untried angle.

At CIP, we tell our students that there are no mistakes—just approximations to the right answer. Each question they ask will get them closer to an understanding of the solution to a problem and each answer they try to make will do the same thing. Your son or daughter will start to understand that everything in life is a question, an answer, a conversation, a technique, or even a game, and in order to move forward in life he or she must begin to feel comfortable participating in this process. Everything is a *relationship*.

I know that students with Asperger's can be successful if they have the willingness to ask questions and the willingness to go to an advisor or tutor to help them figure out answers. Asking for help allows them to feel like "they are" in control of "their" life. Robert's story illustrates how powerful self-advocacy can be. His learned ability to get what he needed, to ask questions, and his determination to use resources to find answers led him to creating a productive and successful life for himself.

Residential life—move-in day

Another important cut to "the steel umbilical" takes place on the day your son or daughter leaves home and moves in to a dorm or apartment. Living on one's own is challenging for any young adult who reaches college age. For students on the autism spectrum it is doubly so. On "move-in" day, your son or daughter will meet with his or her residential advisor and roommate(s). A short "welcome" and orientation program will be followed by a tour of the campus.

On this important day, an academic advisor will also be waiting to hear from your young adult so that a schedule of classes and learning supports can be coordinated. While the people who offer these services are not "family," the special kind of support they offer will meet your son or daughter's needs as he or she transitions from home to a college campus or college support program. Your young adult will begin to understand that these people and the services they offer are part of the process for learning the problem-solving skills needed to live independently.

Getting the lay of the land and being safe

The campus is generally a safe place for your young person to explore. It is necessary, during the first few weeks away from home, to make smart choices and find appropriate ways to navigate new and unfamiliar places. At CIP, we know these skills need to be taught and reinforced because your son or daughter is probably used to isolating and being isolated. The campus is a smaller version of the larger world, and learning to be aware of campus safety concerns is good practice for navigating safely as an independent adult. This can be something as simple as getting a campus map and taking a walk or a hike with a mentor or friend during the first week away. It is a wonderful way for your young person to get some outdoor exercise and, at the same time, become familiar with all the new physical surroundings.

Venturing out alone into isolated places is not a wise practice. By asking a friend or friends to "come along," your son or daughter learns that there is safety and strength in numbers. This also provides a good opportunity to share an adventure with others who may have similar interests and might be just as insecure about being "on their own" as your young adult is.

Teaching that there are indoor places on campus that are isolated, like the dorm lounge late at night, is important. In daytime hours, these places are bustling with activity; the same goes for the lower levels in the building where the laundry is located. To optimize safety, we encourage doing laundry as a group activity. Planning for this activity with other students who live on the same dorm floor, or in the same apartment, ensures safety. What might be common sense to a non-Asperger's young adult—for example, asking a friend or fellow classmate to walk with one—needs to be taught and then learned by those on the autism spectrum.

Other basics, such as always keeping cell phones charged, programming in emergency numbers, and taking the phone along whenever you are going out, is reinforced daily until it becomes second nature to students. The following story about an outing to New York City is a poignant example of why these precautions are so important.

CRAIG

Craig arrived at our Berkshire Center in the fall of 2009. He was very enthusiastic and likable. Because of ADHD and his Asperger's Syndrome diagnosis, Craig had difficulty listening to instructions, following instructions, or focusing on any one topic for more than a few minutes at a time. He tried very hard; he was always the first student to volunteer to attend or participate in any off-campus activity, social occasion, or sporting event.

Craig and his fellow classmates in the student senate helped CIP staff plan a day trip to New York City for early October. Craig was very enthusiastic during the planning process and participated in creating the itinerary for the day. He loved the theatre and was very excited about the group seeing a "real" Broadway play. He also liked the idea of being in the "City" for the day with his friends and his roommate.

The night before the trip, residential staff helped each student get ready and organized and be all set to go. They made sure alarm clocks (two if necessary) were set and that backpacks were packed. A checklist for the trip was created, with input from the students, that included packing snacks, water, medications, and, most importantly, something to do on the long van ride. As part of this preparation, staff made sure that all students had charged or were charging their cell phone, and that they had all programmed in the numbers of all staff members going on the trip.

It was a fine October morning when ten very excited and happy students and two equally excited and happy staff members boarded the minivans for their big day away. Once the vans were on the road, staff explained to everyone that the students would form small groups upon arrival in New York City. These small groups would stay together within the larger group. Each person gave a spoken verbal agreement to the policy. However, "if," and "in spite of" this rule, someone did separate from the group, he or she would phone a staff member immediately using the cell phone with the numbers programmed in.

Staff did a "check-in" with each student, making sure they all really understood how the day was going to proceed. They also made sure each person understood the importance of staying together. During this check-in, Craig let staff know that he had forgotten to bring his cell phone. Staff made sure Craig knew and understood how important it was for him to stay with a staff member at all times and that this was unfortunately the price to be paid for not having a cell phone.

While purchasing tickets in Times Square, Craig's staff member was preoccupied for a few minutes as she searched in her purse for a credit card to pay for the tickets. When she turned around, Craig was not around her. The crowd was pressing in on the group. Everyone immediately fanned out (in their small groups) to look for Craig.

Initially Craig panicked and I do not think he even fully understood what had happened in those first few minutes away from his group. Then he remembered that staff had given him a written list of all staff numbers "just in case." It took a little while for Craig to find a pay phone (they are few and far between in New York City, in this day and age of cell phones). Happily, he was reunited with his group within the hour.

As scary and nerve-wracking as this was for all involved, this event certainly was one of those priceless "teachable moments." The group learned that, while the planning, preparation, and precautions may seem childish, or unnecessary, they are vital to keeping everyone safe. It took less than 60 seconds for Craig to lose sight of his group. It took almost an hour to find him and for him to be reunited with everyone. Mastering safety awareness, coaching, pre-planning, and knowing what to do if all of the above should fail all came into play on this day.

Other safety awareness skills such as locking doors and not inviting strangers or people your son or daughter does not know well into apartments or bedrooms should be taught. Since your young adult has not lived alone, mentors and advisors will need to reinforce this with examples. Tell your son or daughter that leaving a laptop on his or her desk and without locking the door before going down the hallway to a dorm could be a problem. By teaching your young adult how to use intuition and good social judgment, he or she learns not to trust "just anyone." Friends and acquaintances need to prove to your son or daughter that they are trustworthy over time.

Relationships

At CIP, most of our young people have had little or no experience in high school with dating or building relationships with the opposite sex. They may have had an occasional "date" set up by their parents or perhaps a friend or neighbor from down the street or next door who might come over "once in a while" to watch TV or a movie. At the other extreme, your son or daughter might have felt desperate and hooked up with the wrong person, crowd, or online…just to be accepted. At this stage of development, my staff encourage group activities. This is safer, and gives young adults living on campus a secure and manageable way to start socializing. Another appropriate step during these early days might be asking someone to go to a football game or to study at the library. This sets the stage for developing deeper relationships at a slower and more manageable pace.

If your student has been sheltered from relationships or from socializing at home, he or she may feel the need to make up for lost time. At CIP, we advise being careful, going slowly, and not becoming so absorbed in someone else's attention that they "over-commit." Taking slower steps and building an honest relationship is essential. We help our young adults understand that the best relationships develop from friendships built around common interests. Most of all, CIP staff encourage all of our students to be honest about who they truly are (diagnosis and all) and never to be ashamed of having Asperger's Syndrome, autism, or learning differences. By doing this, we know they will attract people who have similar values and interests.

There are several good books that will help you understand how your son or daughter's learning differences affect the process of trying to form intimate relationships. I learned a lot from *The Asperger Love Guide* (2005), written by Genevieve Edmonds and Dean Worton; it is very helpful, and I recommend reading it before helping your son or daughter to become socially active.

Dating on campus

Over the 28 years that my program has existed, our centers have had many students "date" while they are in our programs. The researchers tell us that young adults on the autism spectrum have an emotional age and level of maturity that is 30 percent less than their chronological age. We know from experience that our students are experiencing junior high (13- to 14-year-old) behaviors in 19- to 20-year-old bodies. It is important that your son or daughter works with advisors, mentors, and support staff at this stage. The young person's emotional age and maturity level is at odds with his or her chronological age.

These young adults see wonderful, serious, and meaningful relationships between teenagers on TV and in the movies and I know how much they want to replicate these in their own lives. I also know that they lack the social understanding to know that they should be making and nurturing friendships first. Parents and those working with young people need to talk about the many types of relationships that exist and give real-life examples. Talk to your son or daughter about platonic relationships—students who are girlfriend or boyfriend without any fireworks. Talk to them about dependent and co-dependent relationships (students who attach at the hip with one individual controlling the other). Talk about how this type of relationship can lead to isolation and not being able to engage with or talk to others. Start a dialogue with your young adult about relationships that are based only on sex or physical gratification. This will lead to discussing what healthy relationships look like and conversations about how healthy relationships tend to be exclusive relationships. Encourage your son or daughter, as we do at CIP, to do a lot of group dating in the beginning.

I can assure you that all types of relationships have happened over the many years that my centers have been in existence, positive as well as negative. I have always encouraged parents to become allies and their young adult's "biggest fan" as he or she navigates dating and forming relationships. In doing this, I have found that most parents are happy that their young adult is in a relationship and that they offer encouragement and appropriate advice. However, there are also some parents who expect CIP centers to prevent their son or daughter from dating. In these cases, we work intensely with the parents and the young people to foster dialogue, open communication, and instruction if necessary in building healthy and age-appropriate relationships. It is unrealistic to think that students on the autism spectrum will not want to do what their peers are doing.

Your young adult needs to have a therapist, mentor, or advisor at the program or college who knows how to give advice in this arena. Navigating dating and readiness for dating are tricky. Your son or daughter will need someone he or she can confide in, seek guidance from who will be non-judgmental, and have his or her best interests at heart. My staff and I also encourage students who want to be sexual to talk to their families about this and to schedule a visit with the health center on campus to obtain safe-sex information. When students do not want to share this type of information with their parents, we make sure that counselors and advisors are there to help them make appropriate decisions. At CIP, we do this in a relationship development class. This class allows trained staff to impart information to help students figure out what type of relationship will be best for them. Safety in relationships is a key topic and we illustrate this through stories and examples of how power in relationships can be misused, and what to do if students find themselves in an unsafe or abusive situation. We stress how important the social understanding piece of the puzzle is in all of this. The following stories illustrate the dating and relationship issues that came up for Lindsay and Brian, and then Steven, as well as the solutions and outcomes that each situation presented.

LINDSAY AND BRIAN

Lindsay, a student from the Boston area, was precocious and very needy. She had been involved with several young men on campus during her first semester, and a young man named Brian was her "latest" male interest. Staff knew that Lindsay tended to control her boyfriends and often did this by calling them on their cell phones day and night. Within a week or so of meeting each other, Lindsay and Brian became a couple and Lindsay began to arrange and schedule all their activities together. Staff noticed that Brian seemed to "like" having Lindsay do all the planning. He also seemed grateful for Lindsay's attention. Brian was, in reality, "OK with," and "happy to" go along with, whatever Lindsay wanted or asked him to do.

Brian began to notice (after about a month of being "led" around by Lindsay) that she became increasingly jealous if he talked to other female students. She also got in the way or became angry when he tried to do weekend activities with his male friends. Brian talked to his advisor and therapist about this. He did not seem capable of doing anything about this co-dependent, power/control situation, so Brian and Lindsay's advisors got together and intervened. A plan was formulated that allowed Brian and Lindsay to spend time together and time apart. Their advisors talked to them, separately and as a couple, about co-dependency and what healthy relationships look like when power and control are evenly distributed, and they were both given support around their individual issues.

Unfortunately, Lindsay resorted to controlling and manipulating Brian. To make things more complicated, Brian would only follow the advice of his mentors and advisors some of the time. It became apparent to everyone that Brian and Lindsay really did not want to follow the plan that everyone agreed "was best for both of them."

Lindsay and Brian stayed a very co-dependent couple during their time at CIP. Brian finished his two-year degree and both he and Lindsay got jobs. They continued to be a "couple," were engaged a year later, and then married. They are still together and appear to be happy.

I always tell this story to parents because it illustrates that, while we can give advice and use our staff and resources to steer students in the right direction, ultimately their choices for happiness are up to them as individuals or couples. Your job as parents, and our job as teachers, advisors, and mentors, is to assist your son or daughter in clarifying his or her goals. We will give your young adult the tools to bring balance into dating and then into subsequent relationships. We will teach him or her how to avoid abuse or disproportionate power/control issues. However, although we offer support, sometimes the age-old saying "you can lead a horse to water but you can't make it drink" often applies.

The following story about Steven illustrates how advisors, mentors, and therapists can help students be open and honest as they discover and explore their sexual identities.

STEVEN

Steven, a 21-year-old student from Kansas, was sensitive and soft spoken. He had difficulty with college-level academics and was socially withdrawn. He was very isolated and had few friends. He internalized stress and suffered from poor self-esteem.

Steven's parents, on the other hand, were accomplished, highly educated, religious people who wanted the best for their son. They were a very conservative, traditional family. Steven's father was a psychologist and his mother was a teacher. They brought their son up in a strict, religious household with many rules and regulations.

Steven was trying to be "a good traditional son" while confiding in staff that he was gay. He told his advisors and mentors that he did not want to reveal this to his family and they respected his wish. He asked staff for understanding and support and received this unconditionally. Steven talked to his advisors often and they helped him find resources for information and further advice.

Steven made a lot of academic progress during his first year at our center. He became more independent, exhibited good decision-making abilities, and gained confidence in his sexual identity. His parents noticed these differences in their son during school breaks and when he came home that summer for his semester break. Steven's independence, confident demeanor, and self-esteem emerged. His parents were threatened by his new self-confidence. They decided to pull him out of CIP's program and the college he had been attending in conjunction with our program. They decided he would go to school in his hometown where they could limit or monitor his social activities and assert more control over his life.

Steven's confidence, his knowledge about himself, and his newly found independence were unacceptable to them. I personally think his parents sensed or perhaps feared that he would continue to gain even more self-direction and continue to go his "own way." I am sure they felt they would lose their influence over him if he remained at a school and in a program that was away from them. They may even have sensed his homosexuality. Giving their son more freedom by being away at school and allowing him to be whom he was meant to be (Asperger's, homosexuality, and all) was more than they could handle.

Steven still keeps in touch from time to time with the supportive CIP staff he worked with and he occasionally asks them for advice. He is still in college in his hometown.

Dealing with alcohol and drugs

Your son or daughter will need to learn to use intuition and good judgment by accepting guidance from those working with and caring for him or her in situations where alcohol or drugs are present. At CIP, we teach the technique of "listening to the inner voice" that is present in all of us, and learning to use what I call a "built-in radar system" (intuition) to detect the best way to stay healthy, alert, and safe. We show our students many examples of how to make smart personal choices even though these choices may differ from what their peers are doing. We teach our young adults to trust their instincts; if it feels uncomfortable, leave the situation and follow up this decision with a conversation with an advisor, counselor, or someone trusted who has their best interests at heart.

Open dialogues, examples, and discussion are very effective in talking with young adults about drugs and alcohol. We also teach about local laws—that is, drinking ages, school zone regulations, and penalties for driving under the influence in the states where our centers are located—as well as the consequences of engaging in these behaviors (addiction, dependence, arrest, etc.). You will want to ensure that this instruction, advice, and support are part of the on-campus or college support program you have chosen for your son or daughter.

Young adults with Attention Deficit Disorder (ADD) and ADHD tend to try to self-medicate by using alcohol or drugs. These substances become their "social lubricants" of choice. For example, young men and women who have poor social skills, or who might be too shy to speak up, become relaxed and humorous with a little help from their friend "John Barleycorn" as they say in Alcoholics Anonymous (AA).

Parents can be easily misled by their sons and daughters when asking questions or talking to them about the frequency and occurrence of alcohol or drug use. Oftentimes, young adults will profess that they "never" smoke, drink, or use drugs so vehemently that their parents are convinced this is truly the case. On the other hand, if your young adult is like I was, he or she might be "rule bound" and feel drug or alcohol use is legally and morally wrong. In this case, your son or daughter will be offended by, and may report, someone who is using alcohol or drugs in his or her presence. Young adults who possess this intense sense of "right or wrong" tend to follow the rules very closely and are deeply offended when their peers break these rules.

Other young people on the autism spectrum who have sensory issues might be "turned off" or offended by the smell of smoke from some drugs like marijuana, or the taste of hard liquor or alcohol, or by the noisy environment where people drink or use drugs.

So, how does this all break down in using drugs or alcohol? What goes wrong? How and why does a young adult with a good sense of right and wrong or with strong sensory issues compromise his or her values and way of being in the world? What do these young people do when a trusted friend or romantic interest whom they respect introduces them to a substance or to alcohol? Peer pressure, dares, or someone intimating that they are less than a man or woman for not trying these things also come into the equation. Sometimes these young people are searching for ways to relax or reduce their anxiety, and they have probably observed a parent or grandparent using alcohol or drugs to relax or get through a tough time. They also see this happening in movies and TV shows. Loneliness, being socially left "out of the loop," or feeling intentionally excluded can have a cumulative effect. At our Berkeley, California, Center, we had a likable but gullible student named Keith. Keith had been diagnosed with ADHD and was socially immature and awkward. In the evenings, he often walked over to a local "eating place" called the SONIC® Drive-In to have something to eat and hang out in the parking lot with other teens.

One night, while "hanging out," a couple of "guys" in a car offered him a ride. Against all teaching from his parents and from mentors in our program, he got into the car. The young men in the car were drinking beer and offered Keith a can of beer to drink. He drank it and they gave him some more. After driving him around for an hour, they took his wallet, let him out of the car in another part of town, and drove off laughing. Luckily for Keith, he had his cell phone, was able to call a residential staff member to come pick him up, and was unharmed.

While incidents like this are very infrequent and even rare, they can occur. Staff will often use Keith's story as an example of how things can go wrong and go wrong very quickly. Keith professed to be against the use of alcohol, tobacco, and drugs, but he was easily led into using alcohol when he thought he would gain "social acceptance among his peers." As unfortunate as this event was for Keith, it was a lesson and one that ultimately worked for good purpose. He learned from this experience that, even though he was of legal age, his judgment and actions were those of someone much younger than he actually was. He learned that his lack of judgment was due (in part) to his ADHD diagnosis and that he needed to understand his limits and limitations better. Becoming aware, being astute, and learning from mistakes are just as hard if not harder for those on the autism spectrum.

In their book *Asperger Syndrome and Alcohol* (2008), Matthew Tinsley and Sarah Hendrickx reflect on the use of alcohol and drugs as a coping mechanism for young adults with limited socialization abilities: "Thus, alcohol works as a numbing device which enables tolerance, integration, acceptance, and flexibility, which the person with AS [Asperger's Syndrome] may not naturally possess. It works, but only up to a point, after which it becomes potentially life-threatening" (p.22).

Handling school, college, or program breaks

Once your son or daughter has settled in and gained a sense of independence, school, college, or program vacation time will be right around the corner. Returning home during this first "break" means that he or she must now combine a new vision of "self" with being under your roof again. In the past few weeks or months, you and I know that your young adult has become accustomed to making decisions without your approval. Schedules, classes, socializing, and even mealtimes have been organized around his or her individual needs. How free time has been spent, or what your son or daughter has done and with whom, has been done without your input. I can tell you, unequivocally, that things will not be the same. This is especially so if your son or daughter is a "first child."

In my case, when my oldest daughter came home from school during her first college vacation break, she let me know right away that she was not going to abide by my 11 p.m. curfew rule. With my own Asperger's traits in full swing, I showed her no flexibility. To my way of thinking, my rules were "my" rules, and she would abide by them as long as she was under my roof. She said:

> Dad, I've been away for three months and you have had no idea what time I am coming in at night or what I've been doing while I have been out, or with whom. So, I am not going to come in at 11 p.m., and you will have to "just deal with it!"

By the time the second, third, fourth, fifth, and sixth child went through this same event, I was able to "go along with this" in varying degrees. The ease I experienced in transitioning our roles seemed to correspond with the chronology of their birth order. I would still disagree with these changes, and I would still try to control my children, but it did get easier for me to see their point of view and to discuss things with them as each child went through the process of separating from me. The most helpful thing that you can do is to have your son or daughter talk to you about "all the new" changes during the first few days at home. Initiate (not demand, as I did) a discussion about old expectations and then talk about the new expectations that you both now have. You will need to be sensitive to each other's point of view without getting discouraged. This is new terrain and unchartered territory to navigate, and both of you are coming at it from different vantage points and perceptions.

Allow your son or daughter to explain how he or she expects you as the parent to act when you are all at home. In return, let your young adult know that you trust the decisions he or she has made in the past few months without you. Come to an agreement that when concerns or conflicts arise you will both be open to sitting down and discussing them.

You can also make a list of the possible scenarios that might develop—such as coming home later than you would like, or spending too much time with friends instead of family. Asking your son or daughter for input and suggesting solutions to these scenarios in a respectful way will ease re-entry. As a result, you may very well find that your student will treat you and your husband with courtesy and kindness.

Your young adult will also be convinced that he or she has grown, evolved, and made many changes, and that you seem to have stayed the same and not changed at all. As a father of six, I have had this happen with my own children and I tell them, "Well guess what, nothing stays the same, life is always about changes, you are just not aware of mine." Your son or daughter will need to take the time to see the changes in you as well—after all, you are no longer calling him or her 10 or 20 times a day, right? At some point, your student will comment about some of these positive changes in you, even if he or she has to finesse the situation a bit.

The better the communication your son or daughter has with you, the more you will both end up on "the same page or wavelength." Take the time to let your young adult know how much he or she has grown up, and state positively and with emotion that everyone still needs each other and always will. The changes that are happening mean that you will just need each other in different ways.

When your son or daughter returns to school after having been at home for a while, some of the same feelings that surfaced when he or she first went away to school may resurface. Tell your young adult to allow time to resettle back into the school routine and to re-establish important connections with peers, mentors, and advisors.

Cutting "the steel umbilical" is a vital and necessary process that allows for growth and independence. I am often reminded of a saying attributed to George Burns: "Happiness is having a large, loving, caring, close-knit family in another city!" Not bad advice!

Chapter 3

Keeping it Real

The Donkey Rule

If you have the dedication, you can reframe any negative belief you have about yourself. It just takes perseverance.

If five people your young person trusts say it is a "donkey" and your son or daughter thinks it is a "horse," tell him or her to use logic and take the opinion of those five people to heart. Explain that the five mentors are probably right and that he or she needs to learn to accept what these five trusted people say as factual and true. Tell your young person that these opinions are based on the perceptions and observations these caring people have made in getting to know and understand him or her. Say (quite bluntly, if you must) that, by not taking this advice to heart, he or she becomes the jack***. This is called and often referred to as "the donkey rule."

The following story about a student named Mark is a very poignant example of learning to use the donkey rule for making hard "life choices and decisions" with the input of trusted friends, advisors, parents, and mentors. It also illustrates the opposite of this scenario—making such choices without listening to the advice of others and entering into situations that are not appropriate or healthy, and then learning from these decisions as well.

MARK

Mark was a student from Montana, an only child, who came to our Bloomington, Indiana, Center after receiving his high school diploma. He was an outstanding piano player and interested in floral work. He had a pleasant disposition and demeanor. It was clear to staff that he was socially awkward and that he had been very sheltered by his parents at home. He lacked social judgment and was in complete denial about needing help in this arena.

Mark was easily "led" into situations he did not know how to handle. For instance, during his first few months at CIP, he met another student named Josh and the two became instant friends. At first, this seemed all right with staff because Mark was very happy having a friend who wanted to spend time with him. Mark asked to share an apartment with Josh. Mark talked with his advisor about the pros and cons of living with Josh. After talking it through, Mark's request to room with Josh received approval. Unfortunately, for Mark and his concerned advisor, Josh turned out to be a manipulative person and a new set of problems developed.

Within a month or so, it became apparent to CIP staff that Mark was doing all the cleaning, cooking, and upkeep of the shared apartment. After further investigation, they also realized that Mark was cleaning Josh's room for him, doing his laundry, giving him money, and doing his bidding. Mark denied that Josh was manipulating him sexually. My staff counseled Mark about this in spite of his protests, making him aware of what an abusive sexual relationship might look like and how to stay safe if Josh was sexually and physically harmful.

Mark requested and received a lot of counseling and advice on how to handle the disparity in this relationship, and staff continued to monitor the situation. Unfortunately, Josh continued to manipulate Mark. Staff thought it best to have them switch roommates at this point so that Mark could have a safe space and time away from this living situation. Unfortunately, Josh still pursued Mark and Mark (with 100 percent Asperger's honesty) told staff he was still giving Josh money and wanting, in spite of all advice, to hang out with him. When Josh was not pursuing Mark, Mark was seeking Josh out.

Mark was getting advice about the situation from his advisor, therapist, other staff members, and me daily. He did not seem to be able or want to listen to us, or our advice. Eventually, Josh left the program and we thought the problem was resolved. Mark made a lot of progress after this and started to develop healthier friendships; he took an internship position and began to socialize more with others.

Mark continued working with the staff, gaining confidence in his ability to make the "right" social judgments. It was at this point that Josh invited Mark to visit him for a weekend at his new apartment about an hour away. Mark asked staff, his parents, and his peers what they thought. Each person he asked told him not to go. He ended up in my office at the end of Friday and we discussed the pros and cons of visiting Josh. I asked Mark to tell me what he thought the donkey rule was. He recited it word for word. I then asked him if he thought that his parents, his advisor, his therapist, his tutor, the residential staff, his friends, and I all had his best interests at heart. He said that he thought we did. We talked about the donkey rule together: if five, six, or seven people he trusted and asked advice from said "Don't go to Josh's this weekend," should he follow that advice or go down there? Mark knew the answer but could not accept it.

I think the lure of the attention Mark got from Josh was more than he could handle and he simply could not resist Josh's enticing invitation. In the end, he went to Josh's for the weekend. He chose not to use the donkey rule. Unfortunately, when he returned to campus, he reported to his advisor that Josh had sexually assaulted him. He was embarrassed about the event and refused to go to the authorities or tell his parents. Mark knew he had some healing and a lot of mental processing to do, and he asked his advisor and therapist to help him work through his conflicting and confusing feelings about the weekend.

As bad as this situation was for Mark at the time, he learned from it and used it as a positive turning point in his life. He worked hard to learn what to look for in friends and to distinguish the "good" and "not so good" in people. He began to utilize the advice of others on how to make appropriate social judgments. From that point on, he made tremendous progress, becoming a role model for others by telling his story and stressing the importance of the donkey rule to his peers and new students. He dated a girlfriend, went to dances, and reached out to staff.

A couple of years later, Mark gave a speech at CIP's annual parents' weekend about using good social judgment and learning to trust in the donkey rule. His presentation was impressive, heartfelt, and compassionate. Mark has gone on to do really well and part of this is due to his ability to learn from his mistakes (sometimes, the very hardest way). He now has a job, his own apartment, and, most importantly, the ability to make good choices for himself.

The donkey rule is one of the first things we teach students at all CIP centers. This simple rule helps students make good decisions as they start to separate from their families, and it is part of the self-actualization process. Showing students (by examples such as

Mark's) that they need to ask for input and advice from several trusted people when making decisions helps them build their own sense of social judgment.

I know that young adults on the autism spectrum are often socially disconnected and are overly sensitive to the point that they are consumed with their own feelings and their own version of events. At this same time, they are often oblivious to the effects of their own behavior and ignore how other people think and feel. This creates a skewed vision of the world and impairs their ability to make sound decisions. This is why learning to use the donkey rule is so important.

I cannot stress the point often enough; your son or daughter needs to be working with trained professionals, honest social mentors, compassionate therapists, and competent academic advisors whom he or she trusts. For the donkey rule to be effective, your young adult will need to rely on those whose opinions and perceptions can be trusted.

The donkey rule will help the young person make good decisions as he or she learns to separate from you in a healthy manner. Once this network of trusted individuals is established, your son or daughter will poll four or five people whom he or she respects and know that the advice given will provide guidance in the right direction. At times, your student may want to use you or a sibling for this poll, depending on the type of decision he or she is making. This is completely appropriate. The poll will indicate to your son or daughter what other people, worthy of respect, think, and would do, if they were making the decisions or choices your young adult is trying to make.

In my case, I came to an understanding with myself in order to trust the donkey rule process. If several people I really respected were telling me not to do something I wanted to do, or telling me to do something else instead, I learned that I should listen to them. Over time, and with a fair amount of resistance, I realized that the outcome would be much better for me, even if I still disagreed. Let me tell you about Tim—his story illustrates another example of learning to use the donkey rule.

TIM

Tim, a student at our Buffalo, New York, Center, was a 19-year-old with Asperger's Syndrome. He responded to a job advertisement posted on a campus bulletin board, interviewed really well for a position at the campus bookstore, and was hired for his first part-time job. He was responsible for stocking the inventory at the bookstore. When he told the news to his roommate John, John asked Tim if he could get him a discount on the books he needed for the semester and told him that this would save him a lot of money.

This request took Tim by surprise and caused him distress. He knew (from his first day on the job) that a 20 percent discount was available to him, and him alone, as part of his employee benefits package, and that this discount was considered "a perk" to all employees working at the bookstore.

Tim really wanted to help John but he also wanted to abide by the rules his manager had set. He was afraid to go to his manager about the situation, and the dilemma started making him anxious. Tim decided to use the donkey rule and ask others for advice. He polled his residential advisor and asked a couple of his study partners what they would do. He phoned his dad. He asked the center's Director. Everyone said Tim should muster his courage and ask his manager if he would be able to give his discount to his roommate as a one-time favor and exception to the company rule. While Tim knew instinctively that this is what he should do, the advice of others reinforced this for him. He went to his manager and explained the situation. Tim's manager told him that he appreciated his honesty and understood how tricky this situation was for Tim. He also let Tim know that this rule did not allow for any flexibility or exceptions to it, and that he would have to say no to his request to let his roommate use his discount.

Tim explained this to John and he took it really well. John let him know how much he appreciated his effort to get him a discount. Much to Tim's surprise, at the next staff meeting, his manager praised his honesty to his colleagues and acknowledged to his staff how important it was to abide by the rules even though they can be tricky and difficult. He commended Tim on the way he handled the situation and let others know how much he valued Tim's sense of values and ethics.

The donkey rule teaches flexibility and social judgment. In the situation between Tim and his manager, this rule became a "teachable moment" for Tim and illustrated that honesty and open communication are very, very effective.

Cognitive flexibility and discrepancy theory

The two key components of the donkey rule are cognitive flexibility and discrepancy theory. This section deals with how both come into play.

First, students on the autism spectrum can be extremely rigid in their thinking and lack the ability to compromise, negotiate, or even entertain an opinion that is outside of their belief system. Because of this rigidity, students often try to "go it alone" in decision-making when they encounter problems. Mark's story was an unfortunate example of this rigidity (with a positive outcome) and Tim's story was an encouraging example of cognitive flexibility (with a positive outcome).

I know that young people often lack "workability" and have a difficult time being a member of a team. I also know that they are very gifted in their areas of special interest but highly limited in their ability to interact with others or when working in groups. Unless support and mentoring are given at this stage, this inability will become a liability when a job or relationship is started.

My own cognitive rigidity was extremely high, and as a child I remember reacting badly to my mother changing the living-room furniture around. Every winter she would get tired of the way it looked and decide to rearrange it. She had no way of knowing that this was an emotionally and physically painful experience for me. Everything would be in a new location. This would throw my sense of order, in what I considered my physical space, completely out of kilter. I now know my response to these seasonal changes and to change of any kind is a very typical trait of being on the autism spectrum.

Over time, I began to understand that the furniture rearranging would happen every winter and I made this seasonal event part of my rigid pattern and thought process so that it would be less disturbing to me. Eventually, I learned to like my mother changing the furniture around and I am sure I would have been equally as disturbed if she had skipped a year or two and stopped doing this. I think it appealed to my artistic side to see the furniture in a different display.

However, this acceptance did not carry over into other areas of my life, only the furniture and only in my mom's house. This is an example of how young people with Asperger's, autism, or learning differences have difficulty generalizing any changes. At times, your son or daughter will adapt to change and make it part of his or her own unique thought process so that the change is acceptable. It is critical for the young person to build a coping system that incorporates the donkey rule to handle the many areas of cognitive rigidity where he or she cannot take change, use basic logic, or think "outside the box."

I think the quote "The roller coaster is better than the merry-go-round" is a good example of what I am trying to say. Our students need to risk the unpredictability of the roller coaster versus the routine, stable emotion or predictability of the merry-go-round that takes them in circles, getting them nowhere.

Second, in learning to live with Asperger's Syndrome, I have learned to use what I refer to as discrepancy theory to confront and cope with the cognitive rigidity in me that others instilled in me during childhood.

Discrepancy theory helps young adults see the effects of their behavior on themselves and on others. Discrepancy theory is a structure that helps those on the autism spectrum understand some of the negative emotions they feel toward a person, situation, or event. It addresses the reasons why they might hold conflicting self-beliefs, a discrepancy about themselves, or a discrepancy concerning an action or something they have seen or heard.

This theory describes two different types of self-images that young people on the autism spectrum often have about themselves. The first image is the "actual self" and represents reality and who they actually are; this is the "what you see is what you get person." The second image represents the person that they believe people "in general" or "significant others" think they are.

By the time young adults on the spectrum are college age, they see their peers attaining nice lives for themselves, driving, going off to college, and having relationships. They often feel left out or left behind and they hit a developmental wall. They suspect something is wrong, but will not admit this—to anyone! They simply feel bad about themselves and inadequate, and those feelings fester. These feelings surface with sharp emotional (and at times inappropriate) outbursts, especially if a young person has been bullied, teased, or harassed.

At this stage, things can go one of two ways—young adults implode (go into themselves) or explode (retaliate at everything and everyone). It is my belief that all imploders eventually become exploders—they just take longer to get there. That is what happened to me.

For the most part, I was oblivious to the pain of the many emotional insults that had landed on me during childhood and adolescence. I coped by internalizing these hurts and absorbing them like a "toxic sponge." If you add in the sensory insults caused by my home environment (seven siblings with various diagnoses, illnesses, and parents unable to cope), you get a system overload and a total breakdown. Eventually, all this came spewing out of me one day, like garbage in a trash can that is overfull.

Students on the autism spectrum often look mentally ill because of this overload and their inability to cope. I always compare my own "frontal lobe" with a slot machine with eight wheels spinning at the same time. Each of these wheels is a bio-computer that is constantly analyzing and tracking data. This explains why, when people used to walk up to me and ask me something directly, I might (if on extreme overload) spit out some disparate information that would make them feel like I wasn't paying attention to them, or worse—leave them wondering where my brain was at.

Children and young adults with Asperger's and autism take things literally and try to keep everyone and everything on schedule. When I was a child and the other children would recite, "Don't step on a crack or you'll break your mother's back," I would then go to great lengths to avoid any crack in the sidewalk walking home from school. Every single day, I would reinforce my own cognitive rigidity over and over again. Or, when the teacher read the story to my class about "the sky is falling," I was afraid to go outside in case a piece of the sky might really fall on me. If your son or daughter has many of these misunderstandings (like I did) going on at the same time, you can understand how he or she might present as mentally ill to a clinician, teacher, or therapist.

Your son or daughter may have been the quiet, intelligent student in the classroom who had difficulty speaking up in class (or at home) and being "heard." As parents, you learned to speak for your son or daughter and to answer any questions being asked of him or her. As teachers got to know your child, they probably did this for your son or daughter as well. This in turn caused everyone to be comfortable with your child not having a voice that could be heard above the people who were doing what they thought was right for him or her. The result of this caused "learned helplessness" in your child.

If learned helplessness has not been the result of not having his or her voice heard, an outward affect that on the surface appears to be uncaring, unresponsive, aloof, or uninterested probably is. "Some of us are thicker than others" would seem to explain the seemingly un-phased reaction to any feedback given to an "Aspie." Rigidity is the hallmark of autism and Asperger's Syndrome; we think we "know better" than any parent or advisor and we are not about to change!

I can remember my friend Max trying to talk to me before my divorce, many years ago, about my inflexible thinking and about not wanting to change or compromise. I would not listen and he gave up, finally just walking away from me shaking his head, saying, "You're just gonna run it, aren't cha? You're just gonna run it!" I had no clue what he was talking about. I sure did not think I was running anything, and in my mind I did not even want a divorce.

Many of us with Asperger's Syndrome do not take notice of the normal discrepancies that occur in our day-to-day lives even though they may have occurred repeatedly or seasonally and with regularity year after year.

Neurotypical individuals tend to notice these discrepancies easily and take action quickly. For example, if it has warmed up in the spring, a neurotypical person will realize it is time to stop wearing a winter coat and start wearing a lightweight jacket. An "Aspie," on the other hand, may very well be wearing a winter coat, hat, and gloves because he or she simply has not noticed the difference in weather or even that the season has changed. Friends and teachers have probably asked, "Why are you wearing your winter coat, when it is so warm out?" The "Aspie" will be especially rigid and defensive in hearing this feedback and will continue to wear the winter coat until he or she decides to change it. The following story, from my own life, illustrates how narrow focus and failure to take notice of discrepancies can play out in simple day-to-day exchanges and occurrences.

JIM AND MICHAEL

In 1979, my brother Jim moved to Las Vegas with his wife and children to run a children's group home that I owned and operated. When he arrived, he asked where he should do his banking and I referred him to the same bank that I had been going to for the past four or five years. At that time (the good old days), all banking was done manually and by written check. There were no computers and people interfaced with a teller (usually the same one) week after week.

The next time I went to the bank and gave the teller my check to cash, she looked at it, said to me "Oh, you're Jim's brother," and then told me everything about my brother, my family, and, most disturbingly, my very own life. As I walked away from the teller, I remember thinking: "How did this woman know everything about me and my life when my brother has only gone to the bank once and I have been coming here for five years?" I just let it pass and filed it away in my personal "discrepancy file" (located specifically, in my mind, on the right side of my brain in a little square box) along with all the other discrepancies that had accumulated throughout my childhood and adulthood. I explained it away as simply "Jim talks too much and you can't shut him up."

It was not until years after my diagnosis and a lot of running into walls, isolation, and unhappiness that I finally experienced enough discrepancies to get that "aha" moment of clarity. Having become an astute student after learning about non-verbal and social behavior by reading Stephen Shore's book *Beyond the Wall* (2003), I finally understood that this experience with the teller was crucial to my understanding my Asperger's Syndrome. It slowly dawned on me that I had never once said anything (friendly or personal) to the teller back in Las Vegas for the five years that I had seen her each week at the bank. I had never said, "How's your day?" or "Crazy weather we're having," or anything a non-Aspergian would say. I never learned her name or anything about her life. While thinking about this past event 27 years ago, I decided to try to practice what I was learning from Stephen Shore's book. I guess the saying "better late than never" applies here.

I found myself heading for the Thrifty Car Rental in Indianapolis, Indiana. As I was being driven from the airport to the car rental center, all of a sudden the thought occurred to me that I could say something to the young man who was driving me. Perhaps we could even have a conversation. This was truly a novel thought and something that in the past (remember the bank) I would have considered a total waste of my time. Even though I still thought that I had better things to think about and do at this particular time and place, I was determined to give casual conversation with a stranger a shot.

The first thing I thought of to say was "How about those Colts?" (I knew the Indianapolis Colts had a great football team that year and, even though I was not interested in them and in fact hoped they would fail [I was a Patriots fan], I thought this young man might be interested in them.) We were off and running and then a problem occurred. How would I keep the conversation going? I changed the subject to the weather, then to bicycling (one of my special interests), and then to art museums and famous artwork (which was another special interest). While continuing on our drive, I found out that there were bike paths in Indianapolis I could ride on, and that there were some great museums I could go to. After this encounter, I felt an amazing surge in my self-esteem and a little more competent about navigating the social world around me.

Why did it take so many years and so many "discrepancies" for me to understand this? Why did it take me 27 years to take action? This answer was "brought home" to me recently during a conversation I was having with my friends Jack and Malcolm. They have both known me for more than 20 years before, and after, my diagnosis. Jack said to Malcolm, "Michael has gone from being one of the biggest 'asses' in town to being one of its biggest assets." Malcolm totally agreed. This might sound like severe or harsh criticism to many people, but not to me. It was the biggest compliment they could have paid me (a real tribute to how far I had come in understanding and then learning to modify my behavior, in mastering social competencies, and in achieving the ability to self-regulate).

Change and new behavior are extremely difficult for people on the autism spectrum and it often takes years of role-playing and instruction in social nuances before any of us are willing to change anything or do anything new. CIP's curriculum was developed and designed to break this cycle much earlier in our students' lives. By appealing to a young person's sense of logic and approaching this logic from many different directions such as social thinking, wellness, sensory integration, and cognitive behavior therapy, social nuances become more of a norm for our students. This teaching and subsequent learning is accomplished at daily Reframing classes, held every weekday morning at 8 a.m. at CIP's six centers.

Reframing

To help young adults break out of their habitual ways of looking at things, we hold Reframing classes Mondays through Fridays at 8 a.m. At CIP, we know our students hate to "get up in the morning" for this class, but they soon come to realize how vital it is to attend them. This is where we teach them to look at their lives from a fresh perspective.

A "frame" can refer to a belief, or to a limiting view of the world. Similar to a window frame, the smaller the view, the less your son or daughter will see outside. Reframing seeks to convert your young adult's thoughts and feelings around a negative situation into a positive pathway for change. Reframing identifies the good intention in a negative behavior and readjusts the thought or revaluation process so that behavior will be more successful. Understanding this theory helps your son or daughter re-define experiences and relationships in new positive directions.

In Reframing class, students gain self-awareness by learning how to monitor eating, sleeping, wellness, and interactions using what we call an "emotional thermometer." They learn to assess and look for patterns from the day and night before. For instance, your son or daughter will clearly see the effect eating junk food or food with too much sugar has on his or her body. Students are also able to chart how they feel after 24 hours with no daylight, or isolating themselves on a computer all night long, or going for hours at a time without talking to another human being. By tracking emotions using the emotional thermometer system, our students see that how they are feeling is a direct result of what they have been eating, how long they have been sleeping or not sleeping, and the effects self-isolation is having on their daily well-being.

Your son or daughter will learn that making adjustments to his or her personal emotional thermometer as needed helps emotions to stay under control and social situations to improve. The first steps to making things better might be going for a walk with friends, taking a swim, or going out with a roommate for a meal. By using the emotional thermometer system (I will discuss how to use this system later on in this chapter), your young adult will learn to self-regulate and make good choices.

At CIP, we know from experience that appropriate physical activity and physical outlets lessen stress (anything from taking a jog to a game of pick-up basketball) and that using the student wellness center to work on a personal wellness plan improves the ability to focus on studies. During these individual or group activities, your son or daughter will be in everyday situations that will allow for making new friends. This leads to developing important life skills and that in turn leads to independent living. The stories of Leo and Adam illustrate how Reframing classes helped them gain control of situations they thought were uncontrollable.

LEO

Leo arrived at CIP when he was 19 years old and enrolled at CIP's Berkshire Center right after high school graduation. Leo was charming and likable, and his peers readily accepted him. He got along well with others in spite of his shy self-consciousness. He was tall, extremely thin, a little clumsy, and not very physically coordinated.

In the beginning of the school year, Leo's college homework assignments overwhelmed him to the point of constant anxiety and worry. He had trouble sleeping and getting up for his daily Reframing class before heading to his college. CIP's residential staff helped him get on a more manageable schedule by having him turn off his computer at a reasonable hour each evening, and helping him set alarms to get up early enough so that he could get to his class on time; sometimes in the beginning this meant that staff knocked on his door repeatedly at 7 a.m. Leo needed this extra help until he could get in the habit of getting up, and this help allowed him to function with less stress. He also started working with a therapist and she encouraged him to share his fears and concerns about attending college classes.

Leo was quite oblivious to his emotions and, as likable as he was, he often felt like he was standing in the middle of a minefield when he entered into conversations that had any kind of emotional content or that required him to elaborate on "his feelings." He could not name these emotions to himself or others—for example, what it felt like to be away from home for the first time, or how hard it was to deal with a roommate who was intrusive. Leo also told staff that he had little tolerance for his roommate because he was of a different religion and ate foods he did not recognize or like. He was extremely close-minded and this contributed to his resistance to making or accepting any kind of change.

Leo attended the Reframing class each day with fear and trepidation. He was lucky to have an instructor named Bill for this class. Bill had been on our staff for many, many years, and had a lot of experience with students like Leo. Bill is one of the nicest, easygoing-est (another of my favorite made-up "Michael words") guys in the world. With Bill as his very patient instructor, Leo started to relax and feel comfortable, and was soon able to start naming his feelings and rating them on a daily basis.

Leo was then able to work with other staff members on nutrition, and he learned to prepare and then eat healthier meals. Staff also showed him how to grocery shop and choose healthy food. He learned to have a supply of food in his apartment that he could quickly grab in the morning, and he stopped skipping breakfast. As his sleep improved, he was "more awake" and "present" at the 8 a.m. class and was soon able to participate in ongoing discussions regarding the weekly and daily themes. Remarkably, he started to see the assets that came with his learning difference and learned to self-advocate while being more assertive about what he needed. Daily reframing exercises and readings showed him how to take action and start changing his own behavior.

Reframing class reinforced what Leo was learning in his Bookends class (more on how this class functions later) about using day planners, calendars, and "to do" lists, and the importance of keeping his schedule, cell phone, computer, notebook, etc., in his backpack. He became very dedicated to attending Reframing class because he saw the success he was able to achieve when he tracked his feelings and emotions. He was able to complete several college classes, including some that were very challenging for him, such as an Interpersonal

Communication class that required public speaking. His positive experiences in reframing helped him achieve tangible outcomes. With reframing, motivation, and support from staff, as well as his newly found ability to self-regulate, Leo learned to identify and resolve problems with his roommate and college professors, and to ask for help when he needed it.

ADAM

Adam, a 23-year-old student with Asperger's Syndrome, returned to college after a two-year hiatus and enrolled at CIP's Berkeley Center to learn the techniques necessary to handle all (not just some) of his college coursework and to have the support of staff available to him so that he might be more successful this time around. During his previous attempt at college, Adam did well on his homework and tests but lacked the social skills necessary to complete his group projects. During his first try at higher education, his lack of participation and being able to work as part of a team caused him to withdraw further into himself. He became isolated, anxious, and depressed. Adam dreaded going to classes and felt everyone was purposely ignoring him.

Adam returned to the college thinking he would do better the second time around. He experienced two more semesters of struggling with classes and he earned very few college credits.

During the following college semester, Adam entered CIP's Reframing class with "a big chip on his shoulder" thinking that he knew all the answers and was above all this. Finally, and with much reluctance, he admitted to CIP staff that he needed help in learning how to organize himself so that he could achieve some successes in his new set of classes.

Adam was oblivious to the fact that his lack of the necessary social competencies and his inability to accept help were the two main factors keeping him from this "much wanted" success. There needed to be an inside solution—an acceptance of self—if he was to move forward.

Adam spent some time with his Reframing class instructor reflecting on his unsuccessful experience at school and he agreed to try to start participating in CIP's daily Reframing class, not just showing up for it. Initially he was critical of what was being taught in reframing and seemed to like taking a "devil's advocate" position on each scenario or premise that arose in class.

As Adam learned how to read and track his emotions daily, he came to realize that he had quite a lot to learn about himself. He realized he was "the one" who was shutting himself off and not participating because of his insecurities and unwillingness to be part of a group. He also realized that his classmates back in college were not deliberately ignoring him or "shutting him out."

Adam began to set up weekly goals with his advisor and to track his interactions (or lack of interactions) in "group activities." He learned that his lack of participation caused his group to withdraw from him. Then he set goals to change this behavior. He made an effort to get to know his team members. By offering even the smallest suggestion or helping them in the smallest of ways, Adam saw their response to him change. He then tracked the responses of the group to him when he gave them his full attention and made further suggestions and contributions. He finally realized he had the power and ability to change. He learned (through his once-dreaded Reframing class) that being in a group meant working as a team. He learned that by not participating he was doing a disservice to himself and to his group.

Adam was encouraged when even the smallest contribution to his team led to the team asking him for more input. His ability to "reframe" this situation gave him a new perspective that he could take with him into all his classes every day. Adam then started to engage and take advantage of other models for assistance. He asked staff to help him in understanding and implementing the changes he needed to make, and he started to take our other modules and classes that offered help seriously. Adam achieved academic success and this led to his earning an Associate's degree. He now works in a library where he is part of a team that keeps a small library up and running on a daily basis.

Young adults with Asperger's Syndrome and non-verbal learning disabilities have spent most of their lives struggling to operate within a framework of society that they simply do not understand. "Aspies" are defined as having significant difficulties in social interaction, along with restricted and repetitive patterns of behavior and interests. Therefore, what is known as "normal" to most is a slow learning process for students on the autism spectrum.

My friend and fellow "Aspie," Karen Simmons, founder of the website Autism Today, writes:

> No matter where you are in your journey—whether you experience acceptance or anger; fear or hope; sorrow or joy; now that you have new information, here is the great news. You now have an amazing opportunity at your door to re-frame the core questions you ask of yourself. And "what now?" is a great place to start. (Simmons and Davis 2010, p.214)

By learning and mastering reframing techniques and understanding that negative preconceived notions and expected outcomes can significantly skew the outcome of any situation, students can learn to create a foundation for change and growth. They learn that they can take an active role in contributing to their own happiness by regulating emotions and learning new behaviors through this process.

Adam and Leo learned that the reframing process involves a morning routine and that the sessions are held in a classroom setting or other distraction-free environment such as a quiet room. In this safe, secure setting, instructors guide students through:

- a discussion of the yearly, weekly, and daily reframing themes

- emotional thermometers and discussion

- a discussion of the daily theme and relevant materials

- practice situations (if applicable)

- several hidden curriculum items (the hidden curriculum will be detailed later on in this chapter)

- an executive functioning check to see if everyone is ready for his or her day.

Students are then ready to face their day having learned valuable insight about themselves by becoming aware of their individual wellness issues from the previous evening and getting organized for their upcoming day.

The emotional thermometer

The emotional thermometer provides a visual means into self-regulation in areas such as hunger, anger, loneliness, fatigue, anxiety, fear, disorientation, flexibility, and consideration of others. Emotional regulation is a developmental skill used in interactions between students' basic brain mechanism and their daily experiences with others. At CIP, we teach that the body regulates emotions and helps us react in appropriate ways. The emotional thermometer exercise helps to identify internalized emotions, the first step towards self-regulation.

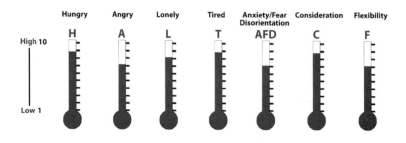

Emotional thermometer

Responses to emotions are monitored daily for the purpose of self-reflection and for gaining insight into the understanding of each student's individual emotional and sensory issues. Through daily self-appraisal, our students can identify the relationship between previous behaviors and habits and track their effect on social and emotional functioning. Awareness is the first step in the process of change. Once your son or daughter understands his or her individual patterns and behaviors, he or she can choose to change them.

The following story illustrates what I am trying to say here—the critical "aha" moment when acceptance leads to insight and the ongoing quest for more knowledge, which then leads to enormous self-change.

EMILY

Emily, in typical college freshman fashion, was always skipping breakfast and heading right to her 9 a.m. class. By staying up too late every night trying to get some extra studying time in, followed by gaming on her computer, Emily often overslept and was always running late. Unfortunately, this scenario happened on the night before an important biology class exam and she barely made it to her class on time the next morning. In spite of a rushed start, Emily was confident that she knew the material that she was going to be tested on better than anyone else did. She had been fascinated by biology since she was a young girl and this was a subject area she always did well in. So why would Emily then fail this midterm? An even better question is, why would Emily not even complete the exam that morning?

Emily was very embarrassed about being "labeled" with a non-verbal learning disorder. She saw the diagnosis as derogatory and inaccurate. She never wanted special help or an accommodation. She did not ask or advocate for more testing time on her exams even though her processing speed was slower than that of a neurotypical college student. She knew that she was entitled to this type of assistance because of her sensory issues, but her own sense of pride kept her from asking for it. Noises during the exam like the ticking of a clock, the shuffling of papers, or the coughs and slight movements of her classmates in their seats were major distractions that would break her concentration and delay her processing speed.

After this biology exam failure, Emily acknowledged that she "might" need some help and asked her advisor to help her learn to self-advocate and cope with this latest setback. She started by attending Reframing classes at CIP (instead of sleeping until the last minute and rushing off to her college classes) and slowly learned how to regulate, listen, and read her emotions using the emotional thermometer system. Slowly but surely, she gained some much-needed insight into what her non-verbal learning differences were all about. As she started to understand and accept her differences and her diagnosis, and see the positive aspects of her personality, she started to deal with her issues in spite of her reluctance.

More importantly, Emily started to achieve the level of success that her native intelligence could produce. By using solutions like self-advocacy to solve her problems in class and at test-taking time, she learned to reframe her narrow perspective into new beliefs. She then started to look at her learning disability simply as a difference, not a disability—akin to speaking a language different from her peers. Next she set about learning the predominant culture's language (the neurotypical language) in order to be successful. She also gained control over her core wellness issues such as hunger, fatigue, and anxiety in order to be ready to face the challenges of each day.

My staff and I know from years of experience that students can learn to regulate their emotions by altering their behavior. We assist students (like Emily) in understanding that they can create the positive feelings they want by altering the factors that contribute to their wellness. Young adults can get a new perspective on how their own regulation (or lack thereof) affects others around them. As students learn to control some of the variables that cause depression and anxiety, they become emotionally more astute and in many cases (by learning these skills and coping mechanisms) they can reduce their need for medications.

Used as a daily process, the emotional thermometer and Reframing classes help connect the dots between students' behavior and their emotions. This can work for your son or daughter too. With practice, he or she can develop self-efficacy and self-control by associating new behaviors with past emotions. Since individuals with Asperger's crave consistency, an everyday 8 a.m. session using the emotional thermometer is an important factor in rewiring some of the complex patterns of the brain. This breakthrough will not be a rapid process because your son or daughter will work with weekly themes incorporated and coordinated with his or her daily lesson plans. Time and practice lead toward wellness and independence. The following topics are related to core issues that should be an important part of any assistance program your son or daughter participates in: flexibility and overcoming rigidity, building relationships, understanding and acceptance of self, understanding individual learning styles, emotional regulation, co-regulation, self-advocacy skills, and self-disclosure skills.

The hidden curriculum

The term "hidden curriculum" describes the unwritten social rules and sets of expectations for behavior in society that most of us adhere to. Richard Lavoie (a CIP Professional Advisory Board member), cited in Bieber (1994), described the hidden curriculum as "the important social skills that everyone knows, but no one is taught. This includes assumed rules, adult and student expectations, idioms, and metaphors" (p.84). Understanding the hidden curriculum is difficult for everyone, but it is especially so for individuals with a deficit in social interaction. It is almost as though there is a secret language neurotypicals use that is not apparent to individuals on the autism spectrum.

A scenario that Brenda Smith Myles, co-author of *The Hidden Curriculum: Practical Solutions for Understanding Unstated Rules in Social Situations* (Smith Myles, Trautman and Schelvan 2004), talks about when lecturing on the hidden curriculum is of a young man with Asperger's Syndrome using a public men's bathroom. No one ever specifically tells young boys or young men the rules of operation, so to speak, for using the men's room. Boys and men (not on the spectrum) instinctively know the answer to the following question: If there are seven urinals and there is a man using the far left urinal, where would the next man coming into the bathroom go? The unwritten answer is the far right urinal. If a third man comes in to the bathroom, which urinal would he use? He would go to the middle urinal of the seven. The unwritten rule is that each person keeps a respectful distance, and gets space and privacy.

Because of the way Asperger's and autism work, these types of situations are not always apparent to young men on the spectrum, nor are the many other unwritten rules such as not taking the urinal right next to another man when the bathroom is otherwise empty. Other behaviors, such as not talking to other men or boys, or looking at them or their body parts, need to be taught, practiced, and reinforced. These things are obvious to their neurotypical peers who seem to pick up these cues by osmosis, while young men with Asperger's and autism have to learn the rules one by one. And, if that is not enough of a challenge, they need to learn that there are variations of the rules to use in disparate situations and that these rules also change according to conditions. To add even more confusion to the subject, bathrooms in various cultures operate differently. This is why instruction and mastering these nuances is so very, very important.

I have found that detailed and specific hidden curriculum instruction and practice serve as an effective method of pre-teaching for students with Asperger's and learning differences. For example: the instructor uses topics that are apparent and easily understood by a neurotypical student but difficult for students with learning differences to understand, such as the bathroom example or examples where interpreting rules and instructions can have a "double meaning." The following scenario (while humorous) shows how important this teaching is:

> In the laundromat, the sign instructing patrons to "immediately remove clothes when red light goes out" refers to the clothes inside the washing machine or dryer, not to the clothes you are wearing. This is so the machine will be available for another patron's use when you are done. ("Hidden Curriculum On the Go" [a 2010 AAPC iPod and iPad application])

Hidden curriculum instruction spells out the unwritten rules and allows students to practice specific situations beforehand. All young adults with Asperger's Syndrome need to be taught about societal expectations that include idioms or metaphors; behaviors and actions; assumed roles; non-verbal actions—such as staring or inappropriate touching; and any other topic that may seem like "common sense" to a neurotypical person.

My staff will often use videos or movies to analyze social situations, and sitcoms generally work well. You can try this at home: stop and start a video you are watching together, then see if your young adult can predict what will happen next. See if he or she can notice sarcasm or idioms, recognize facial expressions, and recognize non-verbal communication. At CIP, we have used *I love Lucy* segments, and staff will play a minute or two of the episode and then hit the pause button on the DVD and ask, "What is Fred's face saying to you? What do you think Ricky will do next? What emotion is Ethel feeling?" Most of this would be crystal clear and apparent to an 8-year-old but can mystify a 20-year-old on the autism spectrum. They will often reply, "How would I know that?"

Your son or daughter can use role-playing to rehearse everyday situations, such as taking a book from the library, asking a stranger for directions, or asking another student on a study date. Hidden curriculum instruction is a process that allows for new understanding and new growth. Understanding that context can be viewed in a variety of ways is an important skill for young adults on the spectrum to master.

If your son or daughter does not know the social nuances in life and why he or she needs them, your young adult cannot go forward with confidence and success in the day-to-day interactions necessary for independent living.

Chapter 4

Pulling it all Together

Executive Functioning

The organized rule the world.

I know that young people with Asperger's and autism will feel overwhelmed by all that they are learning and trying to accomplish or master on their first attempts at living independently. Attending college, making friends, learning new skills, and perhaps participating in an internship for the first time can cause anxiety, forgetfulness, and at times disarray and disorder in their lives. In order to be successful at all of these new things, young adults on the autism spectrum need to learn executive functioning skills.

Executive function describes a set of cognitive abilities that controls and regulates actions and behaviors. Executive functions are necessary for goal-directed behavior. They include the ability to initiate and stop actions, to monitor and change behaviors as needed, and to plan future behaviors when faced with novel tasks and situations. Executive function allows people to anticipate outcomes and adapt to changing situations. The ability to conceptualize and think abstractly is where young adults on the autism spectrum need extra instruction and training. Nearly half of CIP's students who have attended college before enrolling in our program have had to leave college because of difficulty in these two key areas that are the cornerstones of executive function:

1. Organization, time management, prioritization, and follow through with their academics and studies.

2. Socialization and organization in their dormitories or apartments.

I was talking with Ami Klin from the Yale University School of Medicine's Child Study Center shortly after a presentation he gave at the Asperger's Association of New England and he said, "Reading the encyclopedia about how to drive in New York City is not the same as doing it." While many of our students know the rudiments of how to study, how to take quizzes, and how to write papers, they have been propped up in a very structured environment (usually with a lot of parental input and help) and without the distractions and freedom that a normal college situation presents. The little things that parents do at home are often the glue that holds these young adults together: providing a quiet study space, giving a lot of one-on-one support, time-keeping, and being regimented taskmasters.

In the next story, I talk about a student named Zack. He went from relying on his parents to help him stay organized, on track, and on time, to learning (as we all do at times, *the hard way*) to do this for himself by asking for help from others.

Zack

Zack came to CIP Bloomington as a first-year student in the summer of 2010. As a college student in the Criminal Justice Program, Zack was a disaster with a capital "D." He frequently missed classes at the Ivy Tech Community College and never got his assignments in on time. He was not forthcoming about his struggles when talking with CIP staff, telling them that everything was fine and all of his work was done. Of course, when mid-semester warnings came out, the truth became evident and Zack could no longer hide from it. He was completely disorganized, but, because he missed so many tutorial sessions, his tutor had to spend many sessions playing catch up, so there never seemed to be enough time to get organized properly. Zack's parents were completely frustrated as was Zack himself. He had a discouraging semester overall.

Come the spring semester, Zack took three classes. He understood the importance of working with his tutor and organizing himself. He attended his Bookends class and almost all of his tutorials. He got an A and a B in two of his courses, but was not happy with the grade he got in his third course. He took two courses in the summer that he passed, and he took the College Level Examination Program exam in Spanish, receiving 12 credits as a result. Now he was doing well. His success was feeding on itself and he was in partnership with staff and seeing the benefit of listening to their guidance. His parents were grateful that they had hung in through the storm and could see him starting to be self-motivated. In the fall of 2011, he made the Dean's list after taking four challenging courses. He did so well that the Monroe County House of Corrections offered him an internship with them the following summer. He was excited to have the opportunity to observe some caseworkers on the job.

Currently Zack plans to complete his Associate's degree in criminal justice in December 2011. He then hopes to transfer to Indiana University to pursue a four-year degree in the same field.

Students away at school for the first time need to be able to create a structure for themselves that works in an environment full of peers who may be loud, distracting, and very active. This process needs to be taught. Young adults on the spectrum, who have not learned or are not in the process of learning executive functioning techniques, will more than likely fail in school and in trying to live independently.

My own journey continues below, and illustrates another example of how someone on the spectrum figures out how to put structure and organization into his or her world in order to cope with chaos, disruption, and external things like noise and clutter. Figuring out what worked best for me took a lot of trial and error, perseverance, and a strong will to overcome obstacles put in my way by a school system and a home life that was not conducive to my needs.

MICHAEL'S STORY CONTINUES...

Growing up in a somewhat chaotic home, I claimed the dining-room table to sit at when doing my homework and drawing. Since I had no desk in my bedroom and it was often too cool and darkly lit for studying, this was the place I ended up at every day.

TV was not quite as developed as it is now; there were also fewer distractions back then and most children (in this long-ago decade) would not have had a problem with choosing this space to study. The problem for me was that this area was also our dining room and it served as a hallway from the kitchen to everywhere else in the house. I had to learn to deal with the constant traffic going past the table and the sensory overload this caused me. Looking back, it was good executive functioning training because it prepared me for being able to seek a quiet space and then to study at the library at college in total peace and quiet.

My dorm room at college was impossible for this task. The noises and distractions reminded me of my chaotic study space at home and caused me to feel the same anxiety I had experienced during my early school years. I found that, if I started to read a book in my room, I would hear all the noises from the other rooms or get distracted by my roommate trying to talk to me. In my case, the rules of the library were perfect for me. Studying there met my needs, because everyone had to be quiet. There were also study carrels where I could hide away and accomplish my work in an atmosphere that fed, not deprived, my senses. There was just enough background noise to keep me awake, but no conversation to distract me. The chair was just comfortable enough to not be "painful," but not comfortable enough to make me go to sleep.

Executive function is the ability to organize and plan, to set and achieve goals, to understand complex and abstract concepts, and to prioritize and manage time. It requires young adults on the autism spectrum to be able to control impulses while self-monitoring behaviors. Students need to learn how to stop and self-reflect and how to create new strategies that work for them in order to move forward.

Learning to use logic and to create strategies and plans to solve problems is the foundation for executive function. Being able to process information while controlling behaviors leads to accomplishing a task. This is not always easy for teenagers with competing interests. However, like most things in life, it creates another avenue for growth.

I know from my own experience the problems that develop because of poor planning or the inability to be on time and meet deadlines. In my case, I had a great deal of difficulty getting started or initiating a task that I did not want to do, and I would do anything to avoid it. I would clean my room, or help others clean theirs, until the last critical minute when I had to do my project, assignment, or task and then I would do it all at once, and right before it was due.

I was messy and disorganized in the way I kept my class notes and important papers. I had no system to take care of this. I also spent a lot of time trying to figure out where I had left off on a project. I purposely ignored information that did not interest me and then, when I needed that information, I did not have it.

Executive functioning will need to be a part of every aspect of your son or daughter's life: from academics to money management, to health and fitness, and in learning how to handle the skills needed for life and work. Your young adult cannot operate a household, a life, or a relationship without learning these basic tenets. As they acquire the ability to create personal strategies and then use these strategies with peers and others, they master executive functioning.

I know students enrolled in CIP programs and other programs like mine have strong intellectual abilities and are usually very fluent in language usage. I also know these young people have great memories and have the ability to focus intently (especially if they are pursuing their special interests). Executive functioning helps them discover that they can actualize their dreams by learning and using skills to carry them out. Without this knowledge and proper support, they may feel that they are drowning in a million different sub-tasks and cannot find their way to the surface.

The story below—while froth with humor—illustrates that even mastery of executive function can be taken to an extreme and that, as with all things, gleaning the skills and organizational prowess that are necessary for everyday coping and living can run amok. We use this example to show our students that, as with all things in life, mastery of executive function needs to allow for flexibility and sensitivity to the needs of others.

EXECUTIVE FUNCTION GONE WILD

When my dad retired, I went home for a visit to my childhood home in New Jersey. My mom met me at the door and I asked her, "Aren't you excited about Dad being retired?" She had a look of weariness on her face. I asked her what was wrong and she said, "Your father is going to drive me crazy, really crazy!"

I began to understand. You see, my dad was a very, very organized person. Now that he had all this time on his hands, he decided to focus intently, and for long periods of time, on the organization and reorganization of the house—an admirable idea that had (by my mother's description and my observation) run amok.

For instance, when I opened a cabinet looking for some canned fruit, I noticed that all the canned goods were neatly arranged in lines, in alphabetical order, and stacked neatly on top of each other. There were labels under each set of canned goods saying what was in each can in each section.

An educator friend of mine said her "Aspie" husband told her—the day after he retired—"That's not the place to put the mug in the cabinet." She finally had to tell him, "It's alright for you to have those rules for yourself, but don't expect me to follow them."

When I went into the bathroom, there was a note taped to the toilet to "Jiggle the handle" and one on the door to "Leave the door open a little bit so the pipes won't freeze." When shopping with my mother, my dad had it down to an organized, precise science: detailed lists were written out with all the store specials noted. To this list, corresponding discount coupons and vouchers were attached. As to the monthly bills, well, my dad's finances were (of course) in impeccable order and he had all his bills organized and the checks written way out ahead of time. These too would have notes attached to them stating what day they were to be mailed so that everything would arrive on or before the assigned date that they were due.

All of these things, you might think, are obsessive, but not too abnormal. My dad, however, took this one final step further and this was the "straw that literally broke the camel's back." It came one day when my mother saw him trying to control the birds that landed in our backyard. She also had a qualm or two about the methods he had devised for keeping cats and children out of our yard.

Adding to all of this the fact that my dad had recently started trying to schedule all my mom's activities made her act and act quickly. She asserted her independence (her way) by not doing certain things he had scheduled her for and doing exactly as she pleased. This became a sort of cat and mouse game. She only did this "once in a while" to show my dad that she had integrity, that he could not decide everything for her, and that she had had enough of his "executive function" control scheme. In time, my dad toned it down a bit and peace was restored.

My dad did leave my mom one last legacy. Shortly after he died, my mother discovered that, "in anticipation" of this event, he had written out checks, addressed envelopes, and saw to it that the bills and checks were ready for my mom to mail out during the time she would be in mourning. He naturally assumed that she might be so "preoccupied" by the mourning process that she might forget to pay them on time. He had her covered, even from beyond the grave.

Bookends

At CIP, we utilize a process called Bookends (referred to in Leo's story earlier), an executive functioning skills group that meets on Monday and Friday every week. It literally "bookends" the timeframe between the days of Monday and Friday, and allows the time in between and on the weekends to be structured and organized. These bi-weekly groups have an instructor and five students. The students sit in a horseshoe around the instructor and several executive function posters are on the wall behind the instructor (see samples at the end of this chapter).

During the Bookends Monday class, students check in on what they have accomplished over the weekend for each of their college classes or talk about what has been going on at their jobs. Some things that might be included during this check-in might be: completing an outline for a paper that is due; how much reading or research they have accomplished; how they prepared for an exam; or how they discussed having time off with their employer. They learn much by seeing and hearing how their peers are organized and sharing strategies with each other. The goal is for each student to have a personalized organizational strategy for college or work and also one for their living space.

After this check-in is done, students plan and prioritize each day for the week ahead by outlining what they need or want to accomplish, as well as how they will do this until the class meets again on Friday. Many of our students seem to have previously operated under Mark Twain's adage: "Do not put off till tomorrow what can be put off till the day after tomorrow."

On Friday, students go over all they have achieved during the week and start planning for the weekend ahead. In between the actual Bookends class days, students have individual tutorials, study halls, and support in any area that is needed. On the following Monday, the process starts all over again.

During a Bookends class, the instructor is teaching executive function concepts from the posters on the wall. These posters serve as a visual reminder of how students need to approach organization, time management, and prioritizing their work. Students learn to implement executive functioning techniques from these interactions with their peers by comparing notes on the ways they have approached their academics or jobs. Bookends classes are effective tools that help students form personal strategies for approaching academics or employment. Jimmy's story shows how he utilized his Bookends classes, his academic tutor, and his peer tutors to help him transition from high school demands to college expectations.

JIMMY

Jimmy was a student from Louisiana who attended our Brevard, Florida, Center. He had some good general social skills, was very polite, and was well mannered. He had been in a learning support program at a private high school prior to coming into our program and had also tried one year of community college in his hometown. With the help of caring teachers who knew him well, Jimmy was able to get through his high school years. When high school ended, he tried college on his own, but, without the support he had received in high school, he did not do well. His parents realized that he functioned best in a small, structured environment with a lot of individual attention. They felt CIP would give him this support and allow him to learn the skills and techniques required for managing school and work on his own.

At CIP, Jimmy was such a "good kid" that he did exactly what staff instructed him to do. With instruction and pre-planning, he learned to care for himself and his apartment really well. He was quiet, unassuming, and rarely asked for help. He preferred to stay mostly "to himself." To help him in this area, staff encouraged him to help others, hoping he would come "out of his shell" a bit and start to engage with the wider community around him. He did this too. He got involved with one of the local churches, teaching Sunday school to elementary students. He turned out to be a very gifted Sunday school teacher and was asked to participate in and help with other youth initiatives and projects at his new church. He gained confidence and a focus that allowed him to begin creating a rewarding social life for himself.

While Jimmy was successful at working on himself socially, he had a lot of difficulty asking for assistance or help with his college coursework. Because he was so mild-mannered and looked like a regular "Joe College," he slipped by his teachers without notice. However, staff knew he had a lot of difficulty getting organized academically; they also knew that he would turn in assignments on time, but that these assignments would often lack the work necessary for a good grade. When Jimmy started feeling depressed and anxious because of this, staff intervened.

CIP's academic coordinator assessed Jimmy using a tool called the Behavior Rating Inventory of Executive Function (BRIEF). The results of the test helped the academic coordinator determine what areas to focus on in the Bookends classes with him. At this same point in time, Jimmy and his academic tutor bonded and formed a strong working relationship. Three main goals were "set" for Jimmy during the early days of his learning to use the Bookends process.

1. Jimmy was to introduce himself to each professor at his school and explain that he had Asperger's Syndrome. He would then talk about how his learning process was different from that of the other students in his class who did not have his diagnosis. His peers at Bookends and his team of advisors at CIP helped him see that self-disclosure was important and very appropriate. Jimmy's tutor knew that he often misunderstood verbal instructions and that he would benefit from sitting up front in the classroom and receiving written instructions whenever possible. Jimmy was encouraged to ask for these accommodations when explaining his learning differences to his professors.

2. Jimmy would work with his academic tutor to learn how to outline his papers and do rough drafts until the work that was handed in was clearly defined and well written. He would master the subject area according to a preset timetable and plan, and then he would present his mastery of content and subject area through his writing. He would then turn in required assignments on time.

3. Jimmy would work with his tutor in Math (a difficult subject area for him) three times a week instead of trying to cope completely on his own.

In Bookends, other students showed Jimmy how they organized their work and how they asked for academic accommodations. Jimmy rehearsed what he was going to say in front of his peers and he learned techniques from them and from his instructor for planning and completing his work on time. He also followed the advice from the posters on the walls and learned to pace himself by planning each study hour, each study evening, and each study week.

As Jimmy's weekly goals changed, he kept on course during the semester and for the first time ever did not get behind in his work. He kept his test papers, handouts, syllabus, and other important class documents in his notebook using a filing system that he was taught in his Bookends class. He learned how to take notes in a visual way, so that he could remember the important points of lectures. Most importantly, he did these things repeatedly until he had a system that worked for him.

By mastering the Bookends system, Jimmy was able to pass his classes during the next semester and, by using this system in subsequent semesters, he obtained a two-year degree. Upon completion of his Associate's degree, he took the initiative and asked to work with the transition counselor at CIP to help him find the right academic and interest match so that he could transfer to a four-year college in another area. In the end, however, he decided to transfer to the Florida Institute of Technology (FIT) so that he could continue to receive support services at CIP one day a week. He continued to use the techniques he learned at Bookends while attending FIT and checked in weekly with his CIP advisor for assistance in any areas that needed reinforcing or if he started to backslide with his organizational and study skills.

The skills CIP students master in Bookends proceed from academic preparation to career preparation by the creation of one or more portfolios to aid in interviewing, and to visually highlight the skills, attributes, and abilities of students on the spectrum as they start the job search process.

Strategies for life and work…more steps toward independence

As I mentioned earlier, your son or daughter needs to develop personal, academic, and employment strategies while attending college or during career training. At this stage he or she also starts to focus on strategies for independent residential living once college is over. These are skills for life and work. As students learn to prioritize tasks and communicate effectively, they prepare for this new level of independence.

Developing self-monitored organizational skills and follow through are some of the personal strategies to start mastering— starting with personal living spaces. Some students will use color-coded bins to put shoes, clothing, and other items in to stay organized in their rooms. Others use checklists or reminders taped on their bathroom mirrors. Students might also use several alarm clocks to wake up in the morning, or program reminders on their BlackBerrys® throughout the day to help them stay on schedule. My staff and I tell them that any system that works and is used on an everyday basis is a good system.

For instance, I have a system for remembering things that has worked for me for many years. I put notes in my right pocket and I pull these notes out and read them several times a day. If something is more important, I put the note in my shirt pocket where I will feel the paper through my shirt and this is a cue to me to check the contents of this pocket more often. If I absolutely have to remember something, I will use a pen to write some initials representing it on my hand, or have my cell phone alarm go off right before I need to do something. This is a good example of an effective system and strategy that help me stay on task throughout the day and keep me moving from one task to the other in order of importance.

At CIP, a holistic approach is used. We know that getting organized, being on time, and having a routine or schedule that keeps our students on track during the day is a good thing. We also know that these activities need to be included in an overall wellness and sensory integration plan. Students who have strong academic and executive function abilities and strategies need to have a healthy diet, good sleep hygiene, regular exercise, and a sensible self-care routine. Self-awareness and self-regulation are part of CIP's holistic strategy for achieving independence and being successful at work.

Once your son or daughter has mastered executive function strategies, developed a wellness routine, and learned to do sensory integration, he or she will be able to self-advocate and this will lead to operating with confidence and self-determination.

Executive functioning strategies

General strategies

1. Choose individual strategies that work best for you.

2. Use accommodations available at the college disabilities center.

3. Set up step-by-step approaches toward task completion.

4. Use time organizers, computers, and watches with alarms.

5. Ask for written and oral directions, and oral instruction.

6. Plan and structure transition times and shifts in activities.

7. Use visual schedules.

Student weekly schedule

Time	Monday	Tuesday	Wednesday	Thursday	Friday	Saturday	Sunday
8 AM	Reframing Class	Reframing Class	Reframing Class	Reframing Class	Reframing Class		
9 AM			Sensory Integration	Advising Session	Internship *Red Cross*		
10 AM	Biology Class *Berkeley City College*		Biology Class *Berkeley City College*	Social Mentoring			Exercise at YMCA
11 AM					Internship *Red Cross*		
12 PM	Social Thinking Group	Lunch	Lunch	Lunch		Weekend Activity *Group Hike*	
1 PM	Lunch / Study Hall	Advising Session / Career Counseling	Tutoring	Social Thinking Group			
2 PM	Bookends Executive Functioning	Wellness Session	Career Skills Class	Theory of Mind	Bookends Executive Functioning		Weekend Activity *Six Flags Amusement Park Day Trip*
3 PM		Relationship Development	Individual Therapy		Wellness Session		
4 PM	Menu Planning						
5 PM	Apartment Cooking Instruction	Dinner with roommate	Apartment Cooking Instruction	Dinner with roommate	Grill 'n' Chill Potluck Dinner	Weekend Activity *Disco Bowling*	Laundry
6 PM				Deep Cleaning			
7 PM	Food Shopping	Cooking Class			Weekend Activity *Movie Theater Trip*		
8 PM		Study Biology	Exercise at YMCA	Roommate Meeting			Study Biology
9 PM							
10 PM							

College Internship Program

Academics and employment strategies

1. Use Post-it® notes for reminders over your desk or workstation.

2. Set up Google calendar reminders on your computer or cell phone.

3. Use Day Planner to schedule tasks in and to keep to-do lists in, or schedule a task list and notes on your cell phone.

4. Prioritize a to-do list.

5. Organize all your books, papers, etc. the night before.

6. Keep all items in the same place every time.

7. Keep all items in sections in your backpack: keys, glasses, cell phone, schedule, master notebook system for tracking syllabus, test papers, notes, etc.

8. Verify appointments.

9. Have set times to do important tasks.

10. Working backwards, what time do you need to leave your house? Figure out how to order tasks based on when you need to leave or how long each task will take.

11. Remind students of the time an instructor expects them to put into each course. For each semester hour of instruction, three extra hours should be planned by the student.

12. Set the alarm on your cell phone for meetings or classes.

13. Set time limits for tasks.

14. Use study and performance strategies: Survey! Question! Read! Recite! Review! (SQ3R), note-taking skills, tutorial support.

15. Use mnemonics and flash cards.

16. Tape-record lectures.

17. Use a "Livescribe" smart pen.

18. Use audio books, Kindle, Nook, e-readers.

19. Create a dedicated workspace.

20. Organize your workspace.

21. Minimize clutter.

22. Schedule cleaning and organizing at least once a week.

23. Use repetition.

24. Visualization...see it in your mind.

25. Association—Vygotsky called it "scaffolding."

26. Group or place like items together.

27. Write it down—add a sentence—and you can go back and look at it.

28. Use or create acronyms to remember information.

Budgeting and banking strategies

1. Use QuickBooks daily to keep finances straight.

2. File away bills and receipts in an accordion file.

3. Organize emails in your inbox into relevant email folders upon completion.

Residential strategies

1. Put things back in the same place.

2. Put away clothes by color or style.

3. Make labels of where things go.

4. Use colored bins to put clothing, shoes, or other items to separate and organize.

5. Be on time: "Once I get up, I don't lay back down."

6. Set two alarm clocks away from the bed if necessary.

7. Plan the night before for the next day.

8. Lay clothes out the night before for school or work the next day.

9. Put your grocery list or to-do list on the refrigerator.

10. Use a dry eraser board on your refrigerator to write important notes.

11. Put a Post-it® reminder for your medication on your bathroom mirror.

12. Do specific tasks on specific days (e.g., laundry on Thursdays when you have no classes).

13. Take pictures and tack them to a bulletin board or wall, or your bedhead.

14. Use a morning or evening checklist on your bulletin board.

15. Post photos in your apartment of what an acceptably clean kitchen or bedroom looks like.

16. Post photos in your apartment of what a properly groomed student looks like.

17. Executive function checklists posted on bedroom doors.

Every morning

1. Shower

Mon	Tue	Wed	Thurs	Fri

2. Put on clean clothes

Mon	Tue	Wed	Thurs	Fri

3. Put on deodorant

Mon	Tue	Wed	Thurs	Fri

4. Check hair in mirror (is it sticking up?)

Mon	Tue	Wed	Thurs	Fri

5. Eat breakfast

Mon	Tue	Wed	Thurs	Fri

6. Brush teeth

Mon	Tue	Wed	Thurs	Fri

2 points	1 point	0 points
Completed *on own*	Completed *with staff assistance*	*Not completed/ refused to complete*

Date of completion: _____

No. of points: _____

Example of weekly hygiene checklist

1. **Planning/Prioritization:** Creating a roadmap to reach a goal or to complete a task.

2. **Organization:** Arranging or placing things according to a system.

3. **Time Management:** Estimating how much time one has, how to allocate it, and how to stay within time limits and deadlines.

4. **Working Memory:** Holding information in memory while performing complex tasks; being able to draw on past experiences to apply to the current situation.

5. **Self-Perception and Awareness:** Taking a bird's-eye view of oneself in a situation; the ability to self-monitor and self-evaluate one's thinking process.

6. **Response Inhibition:** Thinking before acting; to consider multiple factors before responding to a situation.

7. **Self-Regulation of Affect:** Managing emotions in order to achieve goals, complete tasks, or control or direct your behavior.

8. **Task Initiation:** Beginning projects without undue procrastination, in an efficient or timely fashion.

9. **Communication:** Sharing information with others via email, telephone, etc. to develop rapport, gain information, or network socially.

10. **Flexibility:** Revising plans in the face of obstacles, setbacks, new information, or mistakes; adaptive to changing conditions.

11. **Goal-Directed Persistence:** Following through to the completion of goals and not being put off by or distracted by competing interests.

"Executive skills" list

- When you feel stuck or overwhelmed...

  ○ Ask for assistance. No one becomes successful completely on his/her own.

- When you get the general idea but misunderstand a few details...

  ○ Ask for clarification. Remember: all questions and all answers are intelligent.

- Communicate with instructors, staff, tutors, family, and friends...

  ○ To initiate a dialogue: smile and say "hello."

  ○ To build rapport: ask them how they are.

  ○ To identify shared interests: tell them about yourself.

  ○ To connect with them: share your struggles.

  ○ To feel supported: ask for assistance.

  ○ To reduce anxiety: ask for clarification.

  ○ To learn expected behaviors: ask them what they expect.

"Communicate for success" list

Chapter 5

Being in the Groove

Social Competency

*People need each other. People need one person to love
and they also need others who love surrounding them.*

What do social cognitive learning differences look like in young adults (aged 18 and up) with Asperger's, autism, or learning differences? Why is it so difficult for young adults on the spectrum to understand them? This chapter outlines the concepts, strategies, and methodologies that guide CIP's practice as we work with our students in understanding and learning the social nuances necessary to function independently.

As Will Rogers said: "Good judgment comes from experience and a lot of that comes from bad judgment." Social fluidity is only gained by a series of miscues and victories, and a whole lot of willingness to practice. Learning the process is more important than focusing on the end result.

"Thinking social"—concepts and perspective-taking

Social thinking concepts allow young adults to focus on "presence of mind." Social thinkers consider the points of view, emotions, thoughts, beliefs, prior knowledge, and intentions of others. Social thinking is synonymous with perspective-taking (considering the perspectives of others). For most people, being able to determine the meanings behind the messages communicated by others is intuitive. Social thinking occurs everywhere, while talking, during walking, and even when reading a book. Social thinking is second nature to most people. It is something that neurotypicals take for granted. As parents, you can understand how difficult this (normally intuitive) process is for your sons and daughters because they are probably hypervigilant: always processing information over and over again.

At CIP, we teach these skills by having our students work with a social thinking instructor individually and also in small groups. By observing the emotions, thoughts, beliefs, prior knowledge, motives, and intentions of the people they are communicating with in a class setting, and taking into account their own feelings while doing this, students learn how to implement social thinking. The skills learned in the classroom, or in a one-on-one setting, are reinforced through visual examples and practiced during social activities and group outings. We also know that you cannot learn social thinking skills by going to a clinic once or twice a week for an hour. Social thinking skills need to be taught and reinforced throughout the entire day and week in all environments and by all staff.

In the next story, I illustrate how coming to terms and reconciling my own beliefs and values in order to accept what others are telling me to do can be frustrating, hard, and rankling. My rigidity and my unwillingness to "compromise" my own sense of "higher" morals and ethics get a real work out as I learn to accept and come to terms with what I need to do to ultimately reach my goals. The story shows how hard this was for me in a society where the egos and needs of others need to be taken into account as I glean understanding of "non-verbal" communication skills and innuendo.

PAPER CHASE

When I was finishing my doctoral dissertation, I was writing my review of the literature on special education. I was basically writing a history of special education until that point in history (1980). When I met with my advisor, he was hinting that it was incomplete and I kept asking: "What is missing?", "Who is missing?", and "Which body of work am I missing?" He finally said: "Professor Kelly has a book." I had been given the book and had dismissed it because it was not significant and was not mentioned anywhere in my review of the literature.

My advisor kept looking at me and I still did not understand what he was meaning. Finally, he said: "You might want to mention Professor Kelly's book in the review of the literature." When I returned with my next draft a few weeks later, I had put a small reference to Professor Kelly's book in my review of the literature (even though I thought it did not belong there).

My advisor again questioned me about it. I still did not understand what he was suggesting. He finally said to me: "You might want to highlight Professor Kelly's book more with the other leaders in the field." I said to him: "He is not a leader in the field; do you want me to lie about it?" He just looked at me and I still did not get it. When I got home, I talked about it with my wife and brother, and they agreed that I needed to do that because Professor Kelly was the Chair of the Department, if I wanted to pass my dissertation.

I was not happy about it and felt like I was bastardizing my work, but I did it. It felt like a forced lie to me and it was hard to do it. But I had worked hard for several years, had three children and a business, and I was not going to allow this to keep me from getting my doctorate.

Non-verbal communication

During social thinking, we teach students to interpret non-verbal communication. Being able to distinguish emotions and infer meaning from the non-verbal behavior of others is key to interacting and acting appropriately on a day-to-day basis. This skill is modeled, practiced, and reinforced daily.

At CIP, students are taught to look at social cues by studying non-verbal behavior. One of the effective techniques we use is having our students watch and observe video clips of *Wallace and Gromit* or *Rocky*. The instructor will stop the video and ask questions like: "What emotion is Rocky feeling right now?" or "What do you think Adrian will say to Rocky next?" This practice starts to "tune our students in" to the completely mysterious world of non-verbal communication and the subsequent behaviors that go with reaction and interaction. Young adults can then learn to dissect what others may be thinking about them, and adjust their reactions to the situation. One of my instructors at our Long Beach, California, Center talked to me about a student she was working with named Wayne. His story is an excellent example of what I am talking about.

WAYNE

Wayne, a first-year student at our Long Beach, California, Center, had been homeschooled for part of high school. He had excellent manners, but often misinterpreted "neutral" facial expressions as "angry." Because of this, he did not want to work with certain staff members at this Center because he thought they were not "smiley" enough (Wayne's description). He equated a person being "smiley" with a person "liking him."

It was determined that Wayne did not need to work on facial expression identification because he could look at a picture or watch a video clip and correctly identify whether the person in question was happy, sad, or angry. For the most part, Wayne's assessment was correct but he would misidentify as mad or angry the neutral expression that some people naturally have on their faces. To help him differentiate neutral from angry or mad, he would need to learn to assess what the person was thinking. He also needed to learn to concentrate on what a person was saying and to listen with full attention (so hard for "Aspies" to do), as well as to look at a person's body language at the same time he was studying his or her facial expressions. He needed to put this all into the context of the environment he was in at the time.

The Long Beach instructor felt that teaching, modeling, and practicing this with Wayne would help him understand what was happening during the social exchanges he would encounter from day to day (especially differentiating neutral expressions from angry ones). However, this classroom plan (while working well with other students) did not work the way she thought it would with Wayne.

In Wayne's situation, teaching him how to implement this strategy actually worked in the classroom setting. But it did not improve his being able to read social situations outside this safe, secure, setting. His instructor was at a loss and then one day, while reading the Sunday paper, she came up with an idea that she decided to try.

She brought the Sunday comics to her next individual session with Wayne. She then asked him to tell her what was going on in one of the comics. He could not do this. (I remember occasionally reading the "funnies" throughout my childhood and not laughing or finding anything humorous. I couldn't understand why people spent so much time reading them—they were boring.) She went over the clues she felt were obvious in the comic strip and then had Wayne read it again. He slowly began to comprehend that he needed to look at the context "and" the environment surrounding the characters and "then" read the comic strip. When he began to link context to environment, he made progress and became much more motivated to see the importance of looking at more than one "thing" in perspective-taking. He was a visual learner. He could listen to instructions and practice in the classroom, and appear to be understanding and gaining mastery in social thinking, but in reality he needed to sit and look at a scenario (in Wayne's case, comic strips worked well) in order to understand fully what his instructor was trying to teach him. Using "visuals" that were not on a TV screen or stagnant (a single photograph with an expression on it) was a way of making things clear to Wayne and it was effective.

The Long Beach instructor realized (with Wayne as a prime example) that some of the ways she was trying to teach social thinking and perspective-taking were going "nowhere" with certain students in her classes. By searching for an alternative, being willing to try a new idea, and then solving Wayne's problem, this instructor paved the way for the light bulb "to light up" for the other students. Seeking alternatives becomes second nature to CIP staff and I encourage them to keep trying new and different ways of imparting the skills for life and work to their students.

Most of our social thinking instructors do have success with TV or video clips of sitcoms when used in the classroom setting, as mentioned earlier. Because of the sarcasm involved in the sitcom plots and between the actors, meaning is lost on most of our students who simply do not understand what is going on. Because they do not understand them, they do not watch them independently when they are with friends or in their dorm or apartment. They turn to their computers instead and will play video games endlessly.

Daniel Tammet, in his book *Born on a Blue Day* (2006, p.157), explains one of the social reasoning differences experienced by those of us on the autism spectrum:

Whenever we visit our friends we usually play a game after supper, such as cards or Trivial Pursuit. Neil says it is good manners to let your hosts win, but I don't understand that because if you know the answer to a question, then why not "go for it."

Personally, I used to get carried away "tagging out" little children during family baseball games. Vince Lombardi said: "If it doesn't matter who wins or loses, then why do they keep score?" My sentiments until recently.

At CIP, we know that this leaves a gap in day-to-day conversation between our students and with their neurotypical peers because they cannot talk about the latest episode of *Modern Family* or *Community*, or even joke about an old television show like *I Love Lucy* or *Gilligan's Island*. Using video clips, the Sunday comics, silent movies, and other sitcoms will help to teach your son or daughter how to use social thinking effectively.

Self-awareness

Young people need to be reminded (often) that they are separate individuals with unique personalities. This is a good thing. They also need to know (and learn to comprehend) that they are living among individuals with many types of personalities (some positive, some not). As they learn that people have outgoing, introverted, exuberant, joyful, or sullen affects to their personalities, they begin to understand self-awareness. Slowly, but surely, they let go of their self-absorption and start learning to relate to people who have personalities that are similar or vastly different from their own personality.

Since students on the autism spectrum often lack an understanding of where they fit in the scheme of things, they have trouble working with others. This is especially so when working in small groups or trying to be part of a team. A good way of breaking this barrier down is to encourage socializing in small groups while engaging with others in a service-learning, volunteer, or community project. This is a safe, secure way to start introducing the concept of "expanding horizons." Having your son or daughter volunteer for "Make a Difference Day" or be part of a service group creating a mural at a school or community center will help him or her to experience inclusion. It is through active participation in these types of activities that CIP students learn to see the needs of others, and to give their time and efforts to important causes and events that encompass a wider community and world. I really like the Martin Luther King, Jr. quote below and try to pass his spirit on to CIP students.

> Every man must decide whether he will walk in the light of creative altruism or the darkness of destructive selfishness. This is the judgment. Life's most persistent and urgent question is: What are you doing for others? (Martin Luther King, Jr.)

Self-acceptance

I talked about accepting a diagnosis in the first chapter. In this section, illustrated by a story about former students Sarah and Gary, I talk about self-acceptance. At CIP, our students begin to learn self-acceptance because it emerges daily through a specific taught curriculum and by working one-on-one with tutors, social mentors, and advisors who value the people they "are" and "are becoming." Through teaching, modeling, and the practicing of necessary social competencies, our students begin to recognize who they really are (unique differences and all) and start appreciating all they have to offer others. Self-acceptance is the key that allows these young adults to gain the self-confidence needed to make significant changes in their behavior. Using what they are learning or have learned instead of comparing themselves with others or trying to be people they are not leads to self-acceptance. In learning to love and accept "who" they truly are, depression and lack of motivation for making changes starts subsiding. In some cases, providing individual one-on-one individual therapy sessions reinforces what they are learning in the classroom setting through activities and in specific programs. It is all about becoming "right-sized" and learning to love who they truly are. Sarah and Gary's story shows two different and successful routes toward the much-wanted and much-valued "acceptance of self."

Sarah

Sarah was a young woman with Asperger's Syndrome who attended CIP's center in Melbourne, Florida. She enrolled in community college classes near our Brevard campus and lived in an apartment connected to our center. The poor self-esteem and lack of confidence that plagued Sarah in high school became acute now that she was away from her home and her family.

Sarah (originally from Rhode Island) was diagnosed with Asperger's Syndrome in her early teens. However, her impression of herself and the one she conveyed to those around her was not her actual reality. She looked like a "regular" student and could do many things well—for instance, she was a wiz on computers—but she had very few friends and hardly ever left her room. In reality, she was insecure and filled with self-doubt and, at times, self-loathing. She would rather be in the false "security" of denial than acknowledging her learning differences.

Because of this denial, the "crisis" that had been simmering during her high school years came to a head toward the end of Sarah's first semester in college. She was floundering, failing half her classes, spending almost all her time in her room alone, listening to music under headphones, and feeling anxious and depressed.

Sarah sank further and further into herself. Staff worked diligently and with a great deal of caring to help her learn more about her diagnosis and try to conceptualize self-acceptance. Her depression deepened and she left our program and the local community college she was attending before finishing her first semester. Despite our best efforts to help her, she returned home feeling tremendously fragile and defeated.

At home, Sarah began working individually with a therapist twice a week. She slowly gained more of "a reality check" about her Asperger's Syndrome and her denial of her learning differences that were linked to her low self-esteem. Once she decided to "resign from the debating society," she came to the conclusion that, in order for her to accept herself, she had to learn as much as she could about Asperger's and then start to work with this knowledge instead of against it.

In the fall of that year, Sarah re-entered our program and returned to her classes at the community college, feeling stronger and wanting to be successful at school and in our program. Once she had a fundamental acceptance of her diagnosis, she made a commitment to herself to learn how to live with it. She worked on her self-acceptance issues and made the most of her CIP classes and programs. She was determined to work with staff and peers, and to use these connections to strengthen what she had accomplished in her intensive individual therapy.

At times, Sarah was still resistant to "some" parts of our curriculum. She knew she could "function" fairly well out in real life by hiding her differences, and this old "coping pattern" was one she would fall back into from time to time. She learned how to link her skills lessons to group activities and then transfer this ability to making friends. She learned how to deal with her academic demands, peers, conflicts, conversations, meeting new people, and managing parental demands by relying on the fact that she had a good mind. Reinforcement from others was a good person, a nice person, and had many fine qualities gave her confidence. She slowly began to understand herself and see the positive aspects of her personality. With this realization, her progress improved. She did well in her studies; she found that she was very talented and accomplished in computers and IT and that people enjoyed her company, especially when she would talk about the latest advances in technology to others. Her enthusiasm for a subject area that she knew really well was infectious.

Sarah began preparing meals and eating with her peers in the apartment dining room instead of eating alone in her room. She implemented the social "small talk" strategies she had practiced during her social thinking appointment. Later that semester, she was open enough to agree to a suggestion from her roommate to attend a CIP student dance. This is where she met Gary, a former CIP student. Gary would often stop by the Brevard Center to reconnect with friends and to interact with CIP's staff. He was slightly older than she was. They connected at the dance, talking about social media she was so good at. Gary and Sarah became good friends.

Several months later, they began to date and Sarah continued to flourish. She grew into a vibrant, self-motivated, confident young woman who was ready to "take on the world." By practicing social competencies repeatedly, she began to build fluidity. Her self-esteem and self-acceptance, coupled with acceptance of her diagnosis, gave her the tools to become functional. The need to "hide" her differences, and who she truly was, no longer existed.

GARY

Much to the concern and consternation of his high-powered, well-to-do family, Gary dropped out of CIP's Brevard, Florida, program after his first year. He resisted his diagnosis of severe dyslexia because, like Sarah, he did not think he was any different from his peers. He was tall and athletic and looked like a "regular college guy"; that was "good enough" for him to disavow being different. He chafed at being "labeled" with a learning difference and he preferred isolation to self-acceptance, or learning how to cope with his dyslexia.

When Gary returned home, after vowing never to return to CIP, things quickly fell apart. Within a few months he was so depressed he would rarely come out of his room. Gary's mother called me in a panic and asked me to talk to him and I agreed.

The next time I was in Florida, about three weeks later, I made a special trip to his home to visit him. At the time, Gary sat in his room night and day playing video games, emerging only to eat the three meals that were prepared for him, and to snarl and snap at the parents who loved him.

I asked Gary if he understood what had happened to him since his departure from CIP's program. I listened as he recounted his resistance to the structure of the program and coursework, his hatred of his diagnosis, his dislike of having to work on social skills, and all of the other things that led to his leaving the program.

I shared with Gary an old Native American tale about a man. "Inside of me there are two dogs. One dog is mean and evil. The other dog is good. The mean dog fights the good dog all the time. When asked which dog wins, the man reflected for a moment and replied 'the one I feed the most.'"

Somehow, Gary understood this analogy and was open to thinking more about specific situations. For instance, I talked to him about his lack of sensory diet and sleep diets (see Chapter 9), as well as his shrinking social world, coupled with his inability to reach out and advocate for himself, and how this had led to him falling further into himself. I pointed out that obsessive behaviors (like playing video games all night long) were making him feel more and more depressed and causing mental and physical decline. I encouraged him to visit CIP, talk with staff, and reconnect with some of the students he liked and who liked him in return. Gary started to relax a little bit. He said he might consider coming to the next CIP dance or perhaps stopping by to visit staff and friends.

As we sat in Gary's enclosed, safe bedroom space, he felt secure and knew he could talk freely and in confidence. He talked about what he had been learning in the program before he left. We talked about self-acceptance, social thinking, the importance of connecting with people, and of course how accepting his diagnosis would lead to progress. He understood the concepts of our program perfectly; he just could not apply them to himself.

While Gary's own analysis of why he disliked the program, his classes, and socializing was impeccable and his logic flawless, he definitely had the structure of the program and an understanding of the techniques we implemented all in his head. He knew how reframing is supposed to work, how socializing and getting to know people would help him with his own self-esteem, and he realized he had failed to integrate all he had learned at CIP into his daily life. I left there thinking how brilliant Gary was, and how he could not see his own feet but he could tell me how to walk.

Six months later I received an email from Gary's mother telling me that he had completed and passed both his college classes that term, was treating them with respect, had a car and a part-time job, and was dating a beautiful girl he had met at a CIP dance shortly after my visit to him (the girl was Sarah).

Gary's mother told me she asked him why things had changed and he told her that he remembered the concepts he had learned at his social thinking appointments, the practice he had done with his social mentor, and the knowledge he had gleaned from his therapist at CIP about his diagnosis, and had started applying them to his life. Sometimes we have to fall down to see the sky.

Flexibility

This is all about your son or daughter learning about being open to new ideas regarding ways of understanding and then dealing with real-life situations. Flexibility allows your young adult to consider another person's point of view. By learning to interpret what others are thinking and feeling, and then allowing for differences between the (often rigid) way your son or daughter thinks and what others think and feel, flexibility is learned. At CIP, we use techniques to help young adults learn flexibility so they can look at a situation from another person's perspective. We use whole body listening and social inference to assist them in forming friendships. Author and autism spokesperson Dr. Temple Grandin says that "many individuals on the spectrum find that becoming friends with somebody on the phone is easier than building a face-to-face relationship because there are fewer social cues to deal with" (1995, p.135), and she advises this as a way to begin to socialize. Young people today are so savvy with texting and managing their lives on social-networking sites that this opens up more opportunity for making friends and finding others who share similar interests than would have been possible even a mere five years ago. They test ideas, try flexibility, and slowly learn that a relationship between two people has to be between two people and cannot be one-sided.

Initiation

Initiation means learning to join in and become an active participant in social activities. It means being able to extend greetings, ask questions, and self-advocate. The process of initiating is practiced with a social mentor in the community taking part in the special interest activity of the student.

The following story was given to me by a social mentor at our Berkshire Center. Clark's mentor initially accompanied him to various activities and was supportive of Clark's interactions with others. As his mentor continued to work with Clark, Clark was able to gain the level of comfort and the social skills necessary to initiate doing activities and expanding his horizons on his own.

CLARK

Clark's social mentor, Dan, speaks:

I have been working with Clark for the 2010–2011 school year. We started this process by working on three goals: (1) Clark will demonstrate independence riding the bus, (2) Clark will decrease incidents of odd physical mannerisms while out in the community, and (3) Clark will engage in relaxation techniques that are appropriate to the environment he finds himself in. These goals were determined in supervision with his social thinking instructor and we worked on them during our social mentoring session each week.

In the beginning of this process Clark was not very open to exploring the Berkshire community he lived in or getting out of his comfort zone. Clark especially had difficulty with the second goal of "working on decreasing odd physical mannerisms" while out in the community even though he was beginning to understand what was considered appropriate behavior. An incident occurred when we went to the student union at the Berkshire Community College campus.

As we stepped onto an escalator, Clark had a moment when he raised his voice and started breathing heavily. I knew this could lead to Clark showing odd mannerisms in public and I also knew that in order to help Clark learn to cope he had to initiate the solution himself. Without this intervention these mannerisms might lead to yelling, hitting, and stomping. I quietly asked Clark, "What could we do in this situation to calm ourselves down?" He thought for a moment and answered: "I could do some deep breathing." We both started breathing deeply and the situation passed with ease. By having Clark initiate the ultimate action that calmed him down, he remained in control and was not judged by me in any way.

Continuing to work with Clark in this manner helped him reach all three goals. After one semester of working on these three goals, Clark was able to navigate his way around Berkshire County with ease. He was able to ride the bus independently to locations around the county. As the semester and our sessions moved forward, Clark's inappropriate behaviors decreased.

Clark was a bright student and showed this continually throughout our work that semester. Clark and I completed a whole unit on community and being a part of something larger. This exercise included going to different locations around the county and taking pictures. These places included the public library, fire station, police station, campus buildings, etc. Clark now realizes that he is an integral part of something away from his own hometown and that using techniques to "initiate" an appropriate change in behavior or being open-minded enough to try something he has not done before has been an important part in the process. The goals we set and the techniques he learned made Berkshire County seem like a smaller town. In his free time, he continues to go out on campus, to restaurants in the community, and movies by himself. Clark will also often invite a friend or friends to go with him.

Reciprocity

Learning give and take in conversations and interactions when sharing with others is another vital skill that young people on the autism spectrum can master. At CIP, we have students practice these in group sessions and one-on-one with social mentors. Working as part of a team and being involved with others during community service learning projects, in classes, and during social and recreation activities gives our students opportunities for practicing reciprocity while being fully supported by their social mentors and other staff who help them when this starts getting tricky or uncomfortable. It is important that students are continuously going into the community to practice in real life their social thinking competencies.

Problem-solving

Being able to analyze, process, and understand social situations and the rules that apply in each circumstance is taught using the same methodologies key to this chapter. Classroom work, working with social mentors, and implementation through initiation or self-motivation are good strategies for problem-solving. To aid our students on a daily basis, we use a great acronym that our students can call upon to analyze social areas when they are not sure how they should go forward or proceed. It is called SODA. This acronym does not replace working with social mentors, advisors, therapists, and staff. It provides a stopgap method until further advice or input from others can be obtained.

This acronym is used by students to help them with decision-making and emotional regulation. When they are not sure (stumped), they need to stop and drink a SODA! This allows them to stop, take a moment to look at what is happening around them, and observe the actions of others and themselves. They can then deliberate about what they might do in the present situation. It also allows them time (while sipping the SODA) to think about what they did in past situations. If possible and if they have the time (especially if it is an important decision), they can poll three to five of their mentors or people they feel use good judgment for input, and then take the action they deem appropriate. SODA allows our young adults to have an improved "shot" at taking the best possible action they can in tricky situations.

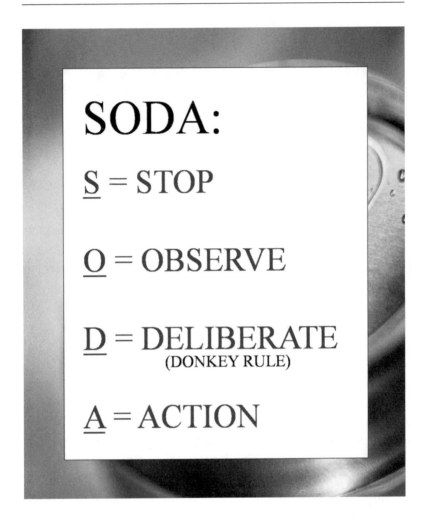

Termination

Students learn how to terminate social interactions in a clear and courteous manner. They practice this in social mentoring, social thinking appointments, therapy, and throughout the other areas of the program. This is another key area that is intuitive to people not on the autism spectrum. It also means knowing when to "drop" something or to be able to figure out when a "line has been crossed," and it is often learned, as it was by Stan and Greg in the stories below, by facing the consequences of one's actions.

STAN

Shortly after entering CIP's Berkeley program, Stan, a very intelligent student from New York, made an appointment at the career assessment center at a local career college for advice and some testing. His career coordinator accompanied him to the testing center and waited in the hallway for him to finish the evaluation. In the middle of the test (about a dozen students were taking it), Stan went up to the test administrator and told him that there was an error on the test and that one of the questions was wrong. The administrator told him to just sit down and finish the test. Stan argued with the administrator and reluctantly sat down to finish the test. He then got out his cell phone (while trying to finish the test), and called his father to tell him about the error on the test. The administrator walked over to Stan and asked him to turn off his cell phone. Stan continued to argue about the question being wrong on the test. A neurotypical person would have probably terminated the confrontation after the first interaction and would certainly have done so after being asked to turn off his or her cell phone.

In frustration, the test administrator asked Stan's career coordinator to come in and remove Stan from the testing room. Stan refused to leave and kept repeating that there was an error on the test. The administrator called campus security. Stan would not leave with the campus security staff and they, in turn, called the state police to help with the situation. The state police arrived and Stan calmly got up and left with the career coordinator. As Stan walked out of the room he said, "I don't understand what everyone is so upset about." He was suspended for the remainder of the college semester.

Stan had a lot of work to do that semester with his career counselor and social thinking instructor to begin to understand how his behavior took the incident to the level of school suspension. He became aware of how his actions and inappropriate behavior in confronting the test administrator, coupled with his defiance about not leaving the room, led to the situation escalating. He worked on learning appropriate termination techniques, the importance of respecting those in authority (through "pseudo situations"), and made progress in understanding when to "stop beating a dead horse" or arguing a point beyond what is considered "a norm."

Stan was able to re-enter his career college (on probation) the next semester and, using what he has learned and mastered, has done really well. He is still quite stubborn when thinking he is right and someone else is wrong, but he has the ability to step back or walk away and rethink his approach to a situation and his reaction to it. He is also learning to listen to the authority of those in charge. The old saying "What doesn't kill you makes you stronger" certainly applies here. Stan needed to experience the consequences associated with crossing accepted lines and expected boundaries in order to start learning about rules and regulations. This incident taught him how things can quickly be misinterpreted by all involved (i.e., the tester calling security and security calling the state police).

Greg

A similar situation occurred with a student from Los Angeles named Greg. He enrolled at CIP's Bloomington Center while attending Indiana University. He struggled with his coursework and received a low grade on a test from one of his favorite professors in a class that he "thought" he was doing really well in. He wanted to talk about this with his professor, and talking to her immediately was uppermost in his mind when he approached her that day.

Greg was a very intense young man with long black hair, a full beard, and an almost fierce look on his face because of his intensity. He worked out a lot at the gym, giving him a muscular and strong appearance. Unfortunately, he approached his young female professor in an aggressive manner without pre-planning what he might say or asking others to help him structure the encounter so that it would be appropriate. He took her by surprise one day after class and asked rather harshly, "Why did you give me such a low grade?" The professor felt somewhat threatened by him, but calmly told him his low test grade was correct and that he had incorrectly answered many of the questions on the test. Greg did not accept this explanation and kept asking her for further explanations. As she began to walk out of the classroom, Greg followed her and continued to ask "why" she had given him this low grade. As he followed her through the hallways, she told Greg to stop following her and that the discussion about his test grade was over. Greg did not comply. The professor called campus security as Greg followed her to the parking lot.

Shortly thereafter, a disciplinary hearing was held and Greg was permanently suspended from college. At this point, CIP intervened and lobbied on his behalf. The College Director agreed with CIP that, under the circumstances, the Disciplinary Board decision was harsher than necessary because of Greg's diagnosis of Asperger's and all that the diagnosis implied. However, Greg's actions were inappropriate, and holding him accountable for his behavior was necessary. The Director explained to the Disciplinary Board that Greg had severe learning differences that caused his rigid thought processes. This rigidity and his indignity about his grade had genuinely affected his perception of what was or was not an appropriate way to handle the situation with the professor that day. Greg received a semester suspension and apologized to the professor for his behavior.

This incident was the motivating factor Greg needed to become open to learning ways to change his behavior and rigid thought processes. He worked hard on learning about perspective-taking and practicing his skills with his social mentor. He now really understood and accepted the boundaries and the limitations of his responses. In retrospect, this incident ended up being a huge catalyst for change for him as he learned, like Stan, how to state his version of an incident, react appropriately, and then terminate the interaction successfully, regardless of whether or not the result was "fair," or he was "right."

Sometimes, individuals need to "hit the wall" in order to accept feedback. Learning to listen, take direction from those in authority, and make a decision to walk away, stop arguing a point, or terminate a conversation is difficult for young adults in general let alone those who are on the autism spectrum. While these are extreme examples, they illustrate my point well. In Greg's case, facing permanent expulsion (reduced to a one-semester suspension) was the motivating factor in changing his thought processes. In Dr. Scott Bellini's book *Building Social Relationships* (2006), he talks about there being a marked difference between teaching social skills and nuances and expecting somebody to perform them. He goes on to say that without providing an actual framework for learning these concepts with examples such as Greg's and Stan's, students will have trouble understanding what the instructor is trying to teach.

Empathy

How do you teach someone the concept of empathy if it does not come naturally? For example, as a teenager I would cry about the holocaust when I saw it on TV. I also cried when Martin Luther King was killed. However, I had (and still have) trouble empathizing with another person's actual day-to-day problems. I also have difficulty seeing things from another person's perspective. Perhaps you see this very same thing in your son or daughter. In order for young adults to empathize and display appropriate emotion, they need to learn to interpret what others are thinking and feeling. Learning to think socially is an ongoing process that needs to be applied throughout the day and week as students use real-life situations to implement what they are learning.

How do you change ingrained patterns of behavior in young adults who are "wired rigidly" and truly want to be that way? At CIP, we approach this as a team. We work with the student using a full complement of trained staff. From the 8 a.m. Reframing classes in the morning, to the residential skills group in the evening, staff members use different methodologies to assist our students with understanding and mastering the wide world of social thinking. In addition to learning skills during structured classroom time, students are given additional support during individual therapy, academic tutorials, advising, career counseling, relationship development, and one-on-one practice of executive function skills and techniques tailored to what they need. Students practice social thinking in activities and in daily living, such as strategies for acting appropriately in the van going to the movies or participating in a weekly "roommate meeting" in their apartments.

Empathy is learned by becoming aware of another person's experience and feelings, and it takes lots of practice for some students to achieve this.

Filtering

When I speak nationally at conferences and seminars, and to students or my staff, I always say that my Asperger's has made me an "equal opportunity offender." Over the years, no one I know has been immune to my "accidental insults." I know that I must consciously work every single day on developing a "filter" between my brain and my mouth—an emotional modulator of sorts.

As a child, then an adolescent, and now well into adulthood, my emotional regulation skills were (and sometimes still are) lacking. I also had (and again, sometimes still do) an extreme "self-righteous streak" that fed (and still sometimes feeds) my belief that people needed (and still need) to hear what I have to say. In my opinion, I was (and am) justified in saying what I have to say, because it was (is) the TRUTH!

My ex-father-in-law used to say to me, "Mike, you are such a smart guy and talented in many ways, so why can't you control your mouth?" I had no answer to this question. I would just stammer and walk away feeling very embarrassed. It seemed like I had only two choices: be an idiot and speak my mind, or shut up. Throughout adulthood, I vacillated between the two with (depending on the situation) very mixed results. Sometimes our students will misunderstand and misinterpret a social situation (as I often do) because they are unable to filter the perceptions and actions of others. In Jeff's story, which follows, he mistook the friendliness and kindness of a classmate for something more. Jeff's lack of social savvy, filtering, and understanding of social norms led to a big misunderstanding.

JEFF

Jeff attended our center in Buffalo. At the start of the spring semester he became friendly with two of the young women who were in his English class at Daemen College. He would talk to them briefly each day saying "Hello" or occasionally talking about assignments after class. When February rolled around, Jeff knew that Valentine's Day would soon be here and he thought that it would be a good idea if he bought two large heart-shaped boxes of candy for them, and he spent quite a bit of money in doing so. He took these Valentine's Day presents to his English class. After class he walked up to the two unsuspecting girls who had been somewhat friendly to him and gave them the candy boxes. He had totally misconstrued the relationship he thought he had formed with them. In his head, he had imagined they were his girlfriends and, because they paid attention to him during and after class, he felt close to them. Both young women were surprised and did not know how to respond to these lavish, inappropriate gifts. They hardly knew who he was. They were very kind to him and then tried to give the boxes back to him, but he insisted they take them. It was awkward for the girls and Jeff simply did not understand what had taken place. He had totally misunderstood the social cues and was ascribing feelings to the situation that simply did not exist except in his mind. He misinterpreted their non-verbal behavior toward him when they smiled and were kind to him.

Luckily for Jeff, another student from our center observed this exchange and mentioned that Jeff seemed perplexed by the girls not wanting his gifts and that his feelings were hurt. I had a talk with Jeff later that day and he had such a hard time understanding why giving such lavish gifts to casual acquaintances was an inappropriate gesture. He had wanted so much to win their approval and did not understand why they did not reciprocate. I could relate to his dilemma. His perspective-taking ability was impaired; he could not understand how they would feel. To his way of thinking, he had built a relationship with them when in reality he hardly knew them. We talked about this at length and I gave my own examples of misunderstandings from my own life. Jeff was willing to work on his perceptions and learn to differentiate fact and reality from imagination. Knowing that this would be hard for him, staff became supportive of his efforts and, little by little, Jeff started to "get it." He learned through practice how to take perspective and check out with others his thoughts and feelings before acting upon them. He learned how to read situations better to avoid misunderstandings.

The social cognitive learning difference is often so abstract and difficult to comprehend that parents are unsure of how to fully understand it themselves, let alone help their son or daughter obtain techniques to master all the nuances. It can "wear down" parents and those around their young adult as they try to deal with teaching this daily.

I remember my girlfriend saying to me, "Michael, it's not good enough that you apologize for stepping on my toes anymore, you need to stop doing it. You know that you are doing this and it still hurts." Alternatively, my daughter would say, "Dad, you know you have a problem with saying things 'off the cuff' to me and hurting my feelings and yet you still keep doing it." Then girlfriend and daughter would say in unison, "Just because you have Asperger's doesn't give you the excuse to keep offending us."

Social appropriateness—the social fake and other concepts

Students are taught a concept called the "social fake" and then learn when it is appropriate to use it. The typical situation is your girlfriend asks you how her dress looks and you really do not like it. A neurotypical would say it looks nice. Young adults on the autism spectrum need to learn to say it looks good. I always had trouble with the "social fake." The other person involved could usually tell by my face and tone of voice that I was not telling the truth. I had my internal moral dilemma going on and I had trouble not seeing this as lying; therefore, I could not hide my discomfort from others. Needless to say, three relationships later, I have become a much better liar, or master of the "social fake."

I know that by this point you could list the incidents or the embarrassing situations you have been put in by your son or daughter's impulsivity or lack of perspective-taking. Young people by nature are myopic. People always talk about "the foolishness of youth," but those on the autism spectrum tend to hold on to this inappropriate foolish social awkwardness much longer and on a much deeper level than those in the neurotypical world. I am sure you will relate and learn a lot from Russ's story. It talks about filter, using the "social fake," and social appropriateness.

Russ

One of my instructors from CIP's Berkeley Center recently sent me this story.

Russ is majoring in accounting at Alameda College. Academically, he does very well, carrying an A to high B average in most of his courses. Nonetheless, his social appropriateness has been a major concern and we at Berkeley have made that our focus with Russ all year. Russ often sounds and behaves like an 11- or 12-year-old rather than a 20-year-old. Russ likes to speak in a high-pitched voice, seems oblivious to the viewpoints of others, tends to isolate himself whenever possible, and resists making any changes. When corrected he becomes upset and ends the conversation abruptly. Russ can be rude and refuses to engage in conversations with others. When experiencing stress he becomes short tempered and agitated. He paces and flaps his arms when especially stressed.

We began the semester by working with Russ on stress management. Since his most socially inappropriate behaviors occur when stressed, staff thought this would be a good way to begin dealing with his inappropriate behaviors. Russ learned deep breathing techniques which he liked doing and used this instruction on a regular basis to calm down. We also helped him implement a wellness program, getting him to exercise at least twice a week and trying healthier alternatives to his favorite foods—pizza and McDonald's. We also had him experiment with some yoga positions and relaxation techniques. Discussions about more effective ways to handle stress such as talking to someone he knew and trusted were helpful. It took Russ a while to be able to implement what he was learning but he did. By the end of his first year at CIP, he was able to calm himself down.

Simultaneously, staff began to praise Russ for all the things he was doing well which usually involved academics but also things like participating in weekend activities rather than staying in his apartment in total isolation. At a "Grill and Chill" (an outdoor eating event) Russ agreed to cook spaghetti and meatballs for everyone and it truly was delicious. Everyone, including his fellow students, gave him lots of praise and expressed sincere appreciation. I think this may have been the first time in his life that Russ felt liked and accepted by his peers. This led him to want to be more involved with the other students.

Another great accomplishment that worked wonders for Russ was our hiking adventure to Rockworth State Park. His mother was visiting for the weekend and joined our van full of students and other staff as we headed out to hike the trails. Russ was clearly enjoying himself and by mid-afternoon was leading the way along the path we were on. His mother was amazed. Her son was actually functioning as the leader of the group. As for me, I cannot tell you how many times I bragged about this to other people in front of Russ. Russ began to understand that changing his behaviors made him a valuable member of his peer group.

As the year went along, it became time to begin talking with Russ more directly about his behavior. Waiting until I had built a relationship of trust with him allowed him to accept what he would have heretofore perceived as direct criticism. Assuring him that I was not criticizing him but wanting to help him go to the next level would sometimes be enough to get him to take in what was being said to him. I began to talk about the need to consider what was important to other people rather than always focusing on what he wanted. This was, and still is, difficult for Russ but he is getting better and better at it.

All staff worked on helping him see how his behavior affected the other people when he was rude or insulting to them. Since Russ really does have a very sensitive and caring heart, he decided to work on this. He has gone from extending his arm in a STOP-like gesture when someone approaches him to being much more tolerant of being interrupted when he is in a conversation with others.

Another big piece of our work with Russ this year has been to help him begin to envision himself as a young man rather than a child, a role he continued to play in order to get what he wanted. I remember the first conversation I had with him about this. I showed him a poster with the word VISION written on it over a lighthouse shining its beam of light out to sea. I told him that my vision for him was for him to grow into a man who could support himself and live a responsible and meaningful life. The look in his eye at my statement was fear. I relayed this clue to other staff members so we could begin helping him grow in confidence and be able to handle various challenges in life. Whether it was a challenging college course or learning how to be more socially appropriate, he had the ability to learn, to grow, and to mature. We all worked very hard to help Russ understand this. Slowly Russ began changing. We worked on the pitch of his voice and it started getting lower and he started to take on more responsibility for his school work, keeping his appointments, meeting with his professors, and dealing with issues with his peers. Social thinking and social mentoring were so important in the process.

ONE YEAR LATER

I just received the following message via email from Russ's professor at Alameda who coordinates a service-learning project that he participates in. The project involved a group of Alameda students traveling to various locations around the community and assisting disadvantaged people with their income taxes. Russ traveled in a van with his fellow students and made sure that he was dressed professionally for the activity in a pair of dress slacks, a white shirt, and a tie.

This is what the professor told me:

Russ did great! I think I mentioned to you when I last reported on Russ that I had him in class last year and that "socially" Russ has come a long way. Moreover, as an added bonus, he definitely is knowledgeable about tax law. He picked up the Taxwise program quickly and was quite professional with clients. At the site in Berkeley, one of the taxpayers talked to him about his son who has Asperger's Syndrome. He went on to say that his son, who is in high school, is doing well and looking forward to college. He congratulated Russ for his fine work.

In my own case, the support and encouragement of mentors (while not specifically chosen for me, or asked or paid to mentor me specifically) were the glue that helped me hold my chaotic, and sometimes traumatic, life together.

MICHAEL'S MENTORS

My mentors growing up were my seventh-grade teacher Brother Rodney and my father's best friend Tony Torntore. Brother Rodney (Kieran Collins) was a young brother who had big ears like me and was the coolest teacher in the school. He made my life fun and I idolized him. I was a shy, quiet kid who had experienced a lot of crisis at home and was fairly isolated.

Brother Rodney showed an interest in me and treated me like his son. He did little things to show me he cared and sort of took me under his wing. He complimented me and encouraged me to play sports and to work on my science project, etc. I learned a lot about the kind of person I wanted to be from him and entered the seminary after one year of high school because of his influence and that of my brother.

Tony was my father's only friend and, even though they rarely spent any individual time together, they respected and liked each other. Tony was a very creative guy who worked in the clothing business in New York for JC Penney's. My dad did the same job for Montgomery Wards. The first time I met Tony was when I was in junior high and my dad let me take off school to take Tony by myself to the world's fair in NYC. I was a good traveler and could navigate the trains and subways to Queens from my house in Central Jersey and, after being at the fair a couple of times, I knew where everything was and how to get there visually, and I was a great tour guide.

Tony became my guide and mentor from that time on. Whenever I returned to visit New Jersey from the seminary, or college, or after being married, my mom had already called Tony and his wife Irene and arranged it for me. She knew I would want to go over and see Tony. Tony let me talk about anything I wanted to talk about and he listened, smiled, and laughed. He would only speak up when he knew I was really off base and could get in trouble and then we would have a debate. I made so many mistakes when I was young but I knew I could count on Tony to steer me straight.

I admired Tony because he was so organized and had his home set up very artistically. He had dishes full of chocolate and cashews, and always the latest technology and art and decorations. His wife was an invalid for many years and he had the whole house, car, etc. set up for her so that she could push a button and operate cameras, etc. Tony was my hero, and I loved him deeply.

The next story talks about Amy's experience with her peers and allies.

Amy

Amy was a student from Vermont who attended our Buffalo Center two years ago. Everyone noticed that Amy showed up to her Social Thinking class wearing the same outfit every single day. During her individual sessions her instructor discussed the importance of changing clothes daily. This was not getting through to Amy, no matter how many times it was repeated, and every day she would come to her class wearing the same pair of pants, blouse, and jacket.

After a few sessions of talking to Amy one-on-one about others' perspectives, listening to compassionate feedback, and even learning how to digest constructive criticism concerning her daily attire, her instructor realized that Amy just did not "get it."

The instructor decided to use kindness and all the compassion she could muster to tell Amy how her classmates and other people perceived her. She gave examples of what other students were saying and thinking. Some thought Amy was not clean and others thought that she did not own any other clothes. Amy still did not believe that others perceived her this way. The instructor sensed that Amy was not threatened by what she was saying and asked Amy if she would be willing to use the "donkey rule" to poll five or six people in her social thinking group and see if the perceptions of others were accurate.

During this poll, the other students Amy talked to let her know how they liked her, but that they were put off and kept their distance from her because they thought that she did not care about daily hygiene or wearing clean clothes. Using the lessons they had learned and social thinking techniques they had mastered, they talked about what they wore to work and school and were compassionate in telling Amy what they thought about her wearing the same clothes over and over again.

Amy was finally able to understand two things:

1. That her peers really liked her and wanted to be friends with her and have her be part of their group; and

2. That she was keeping them at a distance because of their perception that she was not clean.

Amy applied the advice given to her by her peers, talked to her instructor about the compassion and kindness shown to her by all those she polled, and admitted that she needed to take what they said "to heart" even though she still did not fully understand why she could not wear the same clothes every day. The next day Amy showed up for class in a completely different outfit and she continued to vary her clothing from that day on. It took a long time and a lot of work for Amy to become flexible enough to make a change. The lesson to us all is that she did get there in the end, using all the strategies and techniques that our program and her social thinking instructor could give her.

This chapter is so hopeful. The thread of the stories becomes a strong, thick cord and eventually a stronger rope that helps

support our students as they venture forth on their own. The
stories illustrate that, while the lessons leading to learning social
competencies are varied, these skills *can* be taught and learned.
With patience, kindness, compassion, and understanding from
teachers, mentors, and others, your son or daughter can master
the fine nuances of social skills to take him or her through life
and work.

Chapter 6

Having a Shoulder to Lean On

Social Mentoring

Firm arms unite a bond strong and focused. Accepting who we are; giving and learning to receive from each other.

At CIP, social mentors are vital for helping our students mature and learn appropriate communication and socialization skills. We look for mentors who are a few years older than our students. Social mentors are positive role models who teach problem-solving skills by modeling real-life situations. This portrayal allows our young adults to practice and master the social situations that come with becoming independent. By practicing learned skills in real-life settings, our students experience success. As they interact with others in school, at home, or out in the community, they build a strong foundation of the skills necessary for life and work.

For example: practicing reciprocal conversation skills about grocery shopping in a grocery store with a social mentor is much more powerful than practicing a pseudo scenario in a classroom with a teacher. Students on the autism spectrum make so many social misperceptions (or in my case, blunders) and, like me, are often unaware that they are doing this. I am amazed at how clueless I can (still) be about certain things. Mentors work with and help students practice effective ways of learning social competencies.

Social mentors meet regularly with students and work to improve individual understanding in key areas needed for social understanding, getting along with others, and making friends. This is done by having students and their mentors take part in real-world activities, or activities that focus on the mentees' areas of special interest.

CIP mentors are usually graduate students in the process of completing their Doctoral studies in psychology or a Master's degree program in related fields such as special education, social work, or human services. Individuals are selected who have good personal and professional boundaries. Social mentors undergo training and receive support materials and weekly group supervision from CIP's social thinking instructor. During this supervision, the instructor outlines three main social competency areas that the social mentor will work on with his or her student that week. These, plus a list of further competencies, are provided at the end of the chapter.

Getting started

The mentor sets up an initial appointment with his or her mentee and spends some time getting to know him or her at this meeting. The student has the chance to talk about special interests, concerns, and things he or she might like to do to work on one or several social competencies. The mentor and the student will then formulate a plan of what they will do, what they plan to accomplish, and what new things they might try together during scheduled weekly sessions.

The social mentor talks in a clear, concise, relaxed, and natural way about the social competency area that he or she will address with the student on the day they meet. Most often, this involves pursuing a student's "special interest." For example, if the student's special interest is computer gaming, and he or she has difficulty forming friendships, or introducing him or herself to others, the social mentor may suggest that they go to a video store. On the way to the store, the mentor might share a story about how he or she strikes up a conversation with a new person.

The mentor might talk about how to make introductory comments to others. At the store, the student would then attempt to have a conversation while at the counter with the clerk. After the experience, and on the return trip to campus, the social mentor would give the student feedback on what he or she did well and what might need improvement. The activities and social scenarios that take place during each session are constructed and monitored with skill and care. The social mentor presents the information to the student in a light, loose, fun, enjoyable, and relaxed manner. At CIP, working with a social mentor is enjoyable and as stress free as possible.

When I present at conferences around the world, I tell the story of Max and Susan. It is a great example of all that a successful mentor/mentee relationship should be and illustrates, once again, that the methodology and the research behind creating a system like this really do work.

MAX AND HIS MENTOR SUSAN

Max grew up in Bloomington, Indiana, and started attending CIP's program when he was 18 years old. He was quiet and shy and had a lot of difficulty communicating directly and interacting socially with others. He was very intelligent (statistics was his area of special interest) and he maintained a 120 grade point average in his class at Ivy Tech Community College.

Academically, Max did really well. Socially, he would reply to others with one or two words and often not talk at all. That was all he could manage when faced with just about any social situation. CIP staff knew that he wanted to socialize and make friends, and that he did not have the reciprocal conversation skills necessary to do this. This became the number one priority to focus on for his social mentor, Susan.

Because of his non-verbal learning differences, Susan knew Max processed information very slowly and had a hard time responding quickly when asked a question or when trying to answer one. He would think about what was being said to him and analyze it in at least 12 different ways before coming up with what he thought was the perfect answer in stiff and stilted words.

My friend Marcia Brown Rubinstien and I sometimes present together regarding the difference between non-verbal learning differences and Asperger's Syndrome. In her book *Raising NLD Superstars* (2005), she says, "The NLDer's difficulty in transforming visual spatial information into activity creates a delay in response time which is neither typical nor tolerated in modern society" (p.35).

The analogy that I use in my training is that of the Virgin River that runs through Zion National Park in Utah. It was mystifying to me, when I camped along the banks in summer in the high desert, that water flowed continuously. I asked a park ranger and he told me that it takes all year for the snow and moisture on top of the sandstone mountains to seep through and thus create a continuous flow in the river all year round. Not unlike our students, whose thoughts take a long time to flow out but run deep and strong.

After talking with Susan about where they might go or what they might do to try out some new strategies, Max decided that he wanted to explore the Indiana University (IU) Statistics Department during his social mentoring time the following week. Max was thinking of transferring to a four-year program there and this would be a good opportunity to "check it out."

While walking to the school, Susan initiated a conversation about his favorite subject, "statistics!" She then made some suggestions about how they might keep a conversation going with other students or any professors they might meet during the time they were going to spend on campus that day. Susan explained how she would begin a conversation with someone, keep it going, and then end it. They talked about questions Max might ask if they came across another student, and how he might show interest in what the other person was saying. Susan and Max did some practicing on the way by rehearsing introductions, talking about her interests (not just his), and then concluding a conversation by saying goodbye.

When they got to the Statistics Department, Max and Susan introduced themselves to a professor who was sitting at his desk, preparing for his next class. Max was able to ask several questions. He started out by saying: "Did you get your degree from IU? Where did you go to school? How long have you been teaching?" This was enormous progress for Max and a good start. As Susan stood supportively next to Max, the professor seemed to understand (perhaps he had other students on the spectrum or had similar traits himself) that Susan was trying to help him. The professor then asked Max if he knew about the Stats Club, a group of like-minded students who genuinely thought statistics were the "be all and end all." The professor volunteered to introduce Max to some members of the club when and if he enrolled in IU's statistics class and program. Max then initiated ending the conversation, saying goodbye and thanking the professor for his time.

During this two-hour mentoring session, Max formed a relationship with an appropriate role model, worked toward his social competency goals, practiced his new skills in a real-life situation, and was able to enjoy his special interest. As a bonus, he became aware of a social group that would help him take his "special interest" further.

Late last year, as I was traveling by plane to a conference, one of the social mentors from our Buffalo, New York, Center sent me this story. I think that my telling this story in "his own words" will convey the importance of finding mentors with integrity, enthusiasm, compassion, and patience for what they are doing and accomplishing with mentees.

LINDSAY

William writes:

For the past eight months, I've been working with a young woman named Lindsay. She is in her early 20s and has not had or been able to make friends since she was in middle school. Like many students I work with, Lindsay has difficulty understanding how others perceive her. As a result, she has not been able to understand the social feedback necessary to develop interpersonal skills. In the neurotypical world, this feedback from others often comes in the form of subtle cues and nuances and can be positive, informative, or negative. Cues help us make subtle changes all day long as we interact with others.

In Lindsay's case, the only social cues she understands from others are the bold, in your face statements that tend to come in moments of frustration and disgust from peers or parents. These experiences have left Lindsay with a huge lack of confidence. I am trying to help her surmount this hurdle so that we can then tackle other social problems she has.

In helping Lindsay, I knew that I needed to build rapport. This was important especially since she was extremely timid, particularly with men. Once she saw that I was friendly and non-threatening, she opened up and asked me question after question. Our sessions never seemed long enough. It was as though her lifetime of confusion, self-doubt, questioning, and wondering why she did not fit in finally had the "chance to be heard and understood."

During our sessions, we talked much faster than she was able to act. By that, I mean we would talk about how a person might handle various situations but she was reluctant to put herself in those same situations. Her lack of confidence and fears about rejection would overwhelm her. She understood what we were talking about, but she was unable (at this point) to implement suggestions or even practice how she might do this.

I was relentless in giving Lindsay positive feedback in the things I saw her do well (a polite exchange with a cashier or in her consideration in asking me where I would like to go during our sessions). As I got to know Lindsay, I would encourage her to take the steps I believed she could handle such as beginning to get to know other students, or volunteering to help at school events. Sometimes we would role-play a conversation she was anxious to have with a roommate, a peer, or her parents.

Eight months after we began, Lindsay can now watch movies and eat dinner with her roommate (impossible for her before). She has begun to build several friendly and appropriate relationships with both male and female students. She still has a lot of work to do as she masters taking social cues from others, but I couldn't be prouder of what she has accomplished since we started working together. Lindsay's progress has been a result of her being able to relax and get to know me and me getting to know her. Lindsay is now looking at the "bigger picture" and seeing that mastering positive and negative social perceptions from others can truly help her, not hinder her, as she learns to navigate making friends, solving problems, and becoming part of peer, school, and family groups.

You can start this same social mentoring process with your son or daughter. I strongly encourage parents to hire and enlist a social mentor during the primary, middle, and high school years, who will become a strong "role model" for their young adults. A way for you to begin might be asking if your son or daughter's elementary school works with trained social mentors. Many high schools and colleges do "mentoring" as part of their service-learning program by selecting and training honors students to work one-on-one with students with social needs. Identifying mentoring programs and making connections for your son or daughter will prepare him or her for high school, higher education, and being successful socially.

Social mentors can also help with appropriate, timely advice about making friends, dating, and talking about meaningful relationships. Kyle's story was related to me by his mentor Robert and is a very good example of how effective this type of mentoring can be.

Kyle and Robert

Robert speaks:

Kyle and I have been working together for almost two years now. We both came to CIP's Buffalo, New York, Center around the same time—Kyle as a student and me as a social mentor. We bonded at once since both of us are artists and share many other common interests. After a few sessions, Kyle revealed to me that he didn't have a single friend throughout high school. He told me he had a one-on-one aid that followed him to every class from grade school through high school graduation. He felt humiliated by this experience and at having to "stick out as being abnormal" in a setting where his peers were not empathetic and compassionate to such differences. I could tell Kyle had a strong desire to fit in socially, have friends, and especially to be able to begin dating.

Kyle's dating experience was about the same as his high school friendship experience—zero. Later that year, Kyle had met a young woman in one of his classes at the University of Buffalo that he was interested in. Kyle and I worked hard on his social skills and he was able to develop a friendship with her. But Kyle wanted more. Unfortunately, the young woman did not reciprocate, and Kyle was left heartbroken.

In the book *School Success for Kids with Asperger's Syndrome* (2007, p.68), Dr. Stephan M. Silverman and Rich Weinfeld say that:

A more common problem than depression in early development is spiraling anxiety, or the buildup of apprehension that comes from anticipation of complexity or failure, or both. Anxiety can become incapacitation, and persons with AS can shut down and become angry because they simply are on overload and can't cope.

We then spent many sessions talking about dating, all the subtleties, challenges, mysteries, etc. He practiced his social competencies at art museums or galleries. I mentioned to him that my fiancée and I met on an online dating site, and I recommended that Kyle try this too. He took my recommendation, and over the past year, Kyle has been on several dates. Internet rapport has been a very good way for Kyle to start a relationship with someone who shares his interests and allows him to get to know the person before meeting her. Emailing and texting before going out on a date has given Kyle confidence and has allowed him to meet a variety of people. This has expanded his horizons.

Kyle has yet to find a long-term partner, but this is a young man who went from having no friends or girlfriends in high school to dating. During our one-on-one mentoring sessions, Kyle has made incredible social progress. While I feel I help guide the way to this progress, Kyle's motivation and willingness to learn and change and gain necessary social skills along the way makes it a two-way street. Kyle is the one taking the initiative and taking responsibility for his actions and I feel this is an excellent outcome in the social mentoring I do with him.

Mentoring is a caring, compassionate way for your son or daughter to engage and take part in the wider world around him or her. Learning social skills brings self-confidence and self-esteem, and builds a foundation for interactions with others. Learning to socialize is another win–win situation for your son or daughter. You will find (as we do at CIP) that he or she rarely misses a mentoring appointment!

Areas of competency

The following is a sample of three key areas a mentor and mentee might work on during their first few sessions together.

1. Eye contact

    a. Maintain glance towards an individual's face without glancing away for more than 3 seconds at a time.

    b. Defined as looking into the person's eyes when you are talking to someone or when someone is talking to you.

    Discussion questions:

    *   How does it make people feel if they do not receive eye contact?

    *   What is the difference between eye contact and staring?

2. Listening

    a. Maintain eye contact without staring.

    b. Keep body language and posture oriented towards the speaker (lean forward slightly and keep head up).

    c. Engage in reflective statements regarding the speaker's statements; this can include paraphrasing what was said, reflecting on what was said, or asking questions regarding what was said.

    Discussion questions:

    *   How might you change the subject appropriately if you are not interested in the conversation?

    *   How does it make others feel when you are not listening?

3. Greeting skills

    a. Provide a friendly verbal greeting such as "Hi, how are you?"

    b. Use a normal tone of voice.

   c. Maintain eye contact and smile.

   d. Introduce yourself and shake hands when necessary (when you first meet someone or when they extend their hand to you).

Discussion questions:

- What is a normal tone of voice?

- When should your greetings be formal/informal?

Here is a list of further competencies that mentors might also work on with your son or daughter.

1. Starting/maintaining a conversation

   a. Make a comment or ask a question that introduces a topic that both people can talk about.

   b. Give others a chance to participate and include themselves in the conversation.

   c. Ask follow-up questions and make appropriate/relevant comments.

   d. Ask open-ended questions that don't require one-word answers as a means to maintain the conversation.

   e. Keep in mind the environment or who you are speaking to when choosing a topic of conversation.

Discussion questions:

- Have you started a conversation with anyone new lately?

- How might you start a conversation differently with someone new compared with someone you know well?

- What are some good conversation starters?

2. Ending a conversation

   a. Wait until the conversation slows, or you need to leave.

   b. Include a courteous statement such as "It was great talking to you" or "It was great meeting you."

    c. Make a departing statement such as "I've got to get going, hope to talk to you soon."

    d. Initiate a handshake when appropriate (formal situations or when first meeting someone).

    e. Make eye contact while saying goodbye.

Discussion question:

- How can you properly end a conversation if the other person does not slow down or stop talking?

3. Interrupting/joining a conversation

    a. Wait for a break in the conversation (for example, when speaking slows or when the subject of the conversation is changing).

    b. Excuse yourself for interrupting the conversation; for example: "Excuse me for interrupting…"

    c. Ask if you may join the conversation: "Would you mind if I join you?"

    d. Make a relevant statement or ask a question to engage yourself in the conversation.

Discussion question:

- What are some clues to look for that others may give if they do not want you to join the conversation?

4. Following instructions

    a. Maintain eye contact.

    b. Acknowledge instructions by saying "OK."

    c. Perform instructed action in a timely manner.

    d. If unable to follow instructions, verbally explain why.

5. Asking permission

    a. Verbally and politely request the privilege of engaging in an action.

    b. Avoid arguing if told "no."

     c. Say "thank you" if permission is granted.

     d. Politely ask for an explanation if not granted permission.

6. Accepting constructive criticism

     a. Maintain eye contact.

     b. Say, "Thank you for bringing that to my attention."

     c. Defer arguing and remain calm.

     d. Ask for advice on how you can better the behavior being discussed.

     e. Provide a verbal response that indicates understanding of the constructive criticism and that you will work on those areas.

7. Maintaining self-control

     a. Maintain a relaxed posture and facial expression.

     b. Use a calm voice and appropriate voice volume.

     c. Defer arguing.

     d. Engage in relaxation techniques that are appropriate to the environment (for example, count to ten silently, engage in deep breathing).

Discussion questions:

- How do you decide what is appropriate voice volume for the situation?

- What are some environments or situations where it is particularly important to maintain self-control?

8. How to accept "No" for an answer

     a. Maintain eye contact.

     b. Say "OK."

     c. Defer from arguing, whining, or pouting.

     d. If you don't understand why, calmly ask for a reason.

e. If you disagree or have a complaint, bring it up with an appropriate person.

9. Rational problem-solving

    a. Define the problem.

    b. List all possible options/solutions to the problem.

    c. List advantages/disadvantages for each option.

    d. Choose the best possible option.

    e. Follow through with the option.

    Discussion question:

    •   How might you follow these steps if you are problem-solving with another person?

10. Appropriately disagreeing

    a. State your position with rationale.

    b. Defer from arguing.

    c. Listen while the other person or party states his or her position.

    d. If a solution is needed, use rational problem-solving techniques.

    e. Verbally "agree to disagree."

11. Classroom behavior

    a. Attend all classes.

    b. Be punctual.

    c. Bring all necessary materials needed for class.

    d. Wait your turn to speak in class and raise your hand when necessary.

    e. Remain seated unless you notify the teacher you need to leave.

    f. Follow the teacher's instructions.

g. Participate in discussions.

h. Listen and remain attentive.

Discussion questions:

- What does it mean to be attentive?

- What actions are necessary to be attentive?

12. Classroom discussions

a. Wait your turn to speak.

b. State opinions/statements in complete sentences.

c. Stay on topic.

d. Comment appropriately on others' opinions/statements.

e. Maintain listening skills.

13. Making a good impression

a. Maintain eye contact.

b. Smile appropriately.

c. Engage in listening skills.

d. Shake hands when first meeting someone or in a formal setting.

e. Speak in language appropriate to the situation. For example, speak assertively when you want to be persuasive; formally when in a formal situation; and informally when among friends.

f. Maintain an appropriate body posture.

g. Stay on topic while in conversation.

Discussion question:

- How do you know if a good impression was made?

14. Informal language

a. Use when in informal situations, such as with friends and family, or in familiar settings.

  b. Do not use in very formal situations such as job interviews.

  c. Can include slang, and any other conversational terms.

Discussion question:

  • Who do you prefer to use informal language with you?

15. Giving a compliment

  a. Engage in attentive behaviors.

  b. Make a positive statement regarding the other person based on his or her behavior or appearance (for example, dress, hairstyle, etc.).

  c. Avoid inappropriate statements such as those relating to an individual's body or any form of harassment.

  d. Apologize if you realize something was said that makes the other person feel uncomfortable.

Discussion questions:

  • What should you do if someone makes you uncomfortable with a compliment?

  • What is the difference between compliments and harassment?

  • What should you do if you say something that makes another person uncomfortable, and how can you tell that he or she is uncomfortable?

16. Accepting a compliment

  a. Maintain eye contact.

  b. Smile.

  c. Make an appreciative statement such as "Thank you."

17. Entertaining company

  a. Make introductions, if necessary.

  b. Invite guests inside.

   c. Make guests comfortable (for example, with comfortable seating, refreshments).

   d. Notify guests where the bathroom is located.

   e. Use a pleasant voice tone and facial expressions.

   f. Make complimentary statements.

18. Planning what to say

   a. Good when planning for a phone conversation, meeting someone for the first time, or going to an interview.

   b. Make sure to plan statements and areas of conversation that are relevant to the person and setting.

   c. Think of relevant questions to ask regarding the possible topic matter.

   d. Think of how you might leave the conversation. (For example, you have an engagement you need to attend. You could say something like, "I'll look forward to talking to you again sometime soon.")

Discussion questions:

- How many details should you plan on sharing?

- When is it good to have a planned response?

19. Stating an opinion

   a. Make sure to state an opinion as an "opinion," not a "fact."

   b. Make sure you are in the appropriate situation to state an opinion, such as in a class. (Remember: if stating an opinion does not add, or contribute, to the situation, then there is likely no need to express it.)

   c. Make sure your opinion is phrased appropriately.

   d. Defer arguing.

Discussion questions:

- How do you inform others of your opinion?

- Is it OK to disagree with someone?

- What is the difference between a fact and an opinion?

- How do you feel when others force their beliefs on you?

20. Asking permission

 a. Maintain eye contact with the listener.

 b. Ask in a calm and direct manner what you would like permission to do.

Discussion question:

- What are some situations when it is appropriate to ask permission? (For example, using the phone, going out, entering another person's room, borrowing a possession, bringing items into the home, decorating a room, using privileges, or bringing guests into the home.)

21. Reporting whereabouts

 a. Inform those you are responsible to report to of when you are leaving and where you are going.

 b. Indicate when you will return as specifically as possible.

 c. Be prompt and arrive on time for meetings, conferences, scheduled meals, and returning home.

 d. Notify others if you have any change in plans.

Discussion question:

- When is it necessary and to whom is it necessary to report your whereabouts?

22. Calling a friend on the phone

 a. Use skills for planning what to say, if necessary.

 b. Make a call during the appropriate time (typically don't call before 10 a.m. or after 9 p.m. unless someone tells you it is OK).

    c. Avoid making calls when spending time with someone else.

    d. Say "Hello."

    e. Identify yourself (using your name) and where you are calling from (for example, from home or from your place of employment).

    f. Speak in an audible voice tone.

    g. When the conversation is over, say "Goodbye."

    h. Gently place the receiver down; or, if you're using a cell phone, close it quietly.

    i. When leaving or taking a message, make sure it is complete and you obtain the correct information.

23. Personal hygiene

    a. Maintain clean hair that is combed and neat.

    b. Maintain a clean face and hands.

    c. Make sure to be free of body odor and bad breath.

    d. Dress appropriately for social occasions *and* the season; make sure that shoes are clean, socks are clean and matching with no holes, and shirts and blouses and pants are clean, not wrinkled, have no tears or stains, and are color-coordinated.

Discussion questions:

• Does good personal hygiene matter? Why or why not?

• How can I help myself maintain good personal hygiene? Do I need reminders?

24. Respecting others' feelings

    a. Refrain from teasing and insulting others.

    b. Don't violate others' confidentiality.

    c. Don't talk behind others' backs.

Discussion questions:

- What are some examples of insults?
- How can I respect someone's confidentiality?
- What does it mean to "talk behind someone's back"?
- What should you do if you think you were disrespectful of another's feelings?

25. Expressing apologies

    a. Engage in attentive behaviors.

    b. Verbally apologize—for example, "I'm sorry."

    c. Offer to make up for your actions, when appropriate.

    d. Don't make excuses.

26. Respecting others' possessions

    a. Always knock before entering someone's private room.

    b. Ask permission before borrowing another person's property.

    c. Return what is borrowed in a timely manner.

    d. Return what is borrowed in the same condition as when you first received it.

    e. Replace items you may have damaged.

27. Using appropriate table manners

    a. Take small helpings.

    b. Use "Please" when asking for something and "Thank you" when you receive it.

    c. Take reasonable-sized bites.

    d. Chew with your mouth closed.

    e. Use the correct utensils.

    f. Don't use your fingers except when appropriate (chicken, ribs, etc.).

    g. Keep your mouth clean by using a napkin.

    h. Eat at a reasonable speed.

    i. Refrain from belching.

    j. Sit up straight.

    k. Refrain from resting elbows on the table.

    l. Excuse yourself when leaving the table.

28. Completing a task

    a. Begin task with minimal prompting.

    b. Remain on task.

    c. Complete task to criteria in an acceptable time frame.

29. Appropriately asking for help

    a. Maintain eye contact.

    b. Remain calm.

    c. Request help politely and at others' convenience.

    d. Describe the help needed.

    e. Thank the person for helping.

30. Volunteering

    a. Check to make sure the person wants help.

    b. Ask how you can help the person.

    c. Follow through with the help immediately.

    d. Check back after the task is finished.

31. Peer relations

    a. Interact verbally with peers.

    b. Include others in conversation.

    c. Compliment others.

    d. Volunteer to help peers.

    e. Express concern for peers.

    f. Respect peers' rights to confidentiality.

    g. Maintain a positive attitude.

32. Give positive and corrective feedback

    a. Use a calm voice tone.

    b. Maintain good eye contact.

    c. Smile.

    d. Maintain close but comfortable physical proximity.

    e. Describe mistakes in a non-threatening manner.

    f. Describe or demonstrate the appropriate manner in which the task/behavior should be performed.

Chapter 7

Get a Job, Son

Internships and Community Service

Our mission is to graduate young men and women of confidence, character, and integrity capable of making contributions to society and claiming their place as citizens of the world.

TANGLEWOOD TABLE SETTING
8/5/06

Hiring manager to the job applicant: "So, why should I hire you over the other candidates for the job?" Applicant with Asperger's Syndrome to hiring manager: "I don't know how to answer this question because I haven't met the other candidates for the job."

When I was speaking in San Francisco to a parent group a few years ago, two students gave a presentation at a "panel discussion." Both students were about to start their senior year at two different local colleges. Their parents were very proud of them. Both sets of parents had helped their students navigate the process of finding the right professors, obtaining accommodations, and choosing "just the right" courses, and then helped them fill in any gaps with needed support services.

After the informative, well-presented, discussion, I had the opportunity to speak to each student privately and I asked each the following questions:

- Do you do your own laundry?

- Do you cook your own meals?

- Do you drive a car or take public transportation?

- Have you done any community service?

- Have you held a part-time job?

- Have you had an internship in your major field of study?

- Have you been able to form relationships with peers and others?

Surprisingly, both students answered "No" to every question. Both were still living at home with their parents. I also asked each one what they were planning on doing after graduation. One said he was going to graduate school and the other said she did not know. Neither one had a concrete plan, vision, or dream. I also had the opportunity to talk to the parents of each student separately. I congratulated them on all they had helped their students achieve (a true labor of love, dedication, and devotion) and then went right to the point. I focused on all the areas I listed earlier. As I talked to the parents about their young adults, I stressed the importance of letting them achieve independence by encouraging them to live in a dorm or in off-campus housing and not at home.

I explained that, by empowering and encouraging their young adults to do their own laundry, grocery shopping, and cooking, further (and, much needed) independence would be gained. Once each had mastered basic living skills, the next very important step would be finding and then attaining a volunteering opportunity or an internship program that would align nicely with their college major or career interest area.

I also talked to the parents about the importance of creating career portfolios. Dr. Temple Grandin often talks about students creating portfolios of their work in order to "sell" themselves. In her movie, *Temple Grandin* (2010), there is a scene that I encourage parents and their young adults to view. This is the part where she brings her sketches to the meat-processing plant managers she is being interviewed by and visually shows them her work. Her detailed sketches (true works of art) showed the people she was meeting with what she was capable of.

Temple knew she was socially awkward and not the best of speakers. She also knew that if she could convey what she wanted to say visually the managers just might "get it." They did. As they viewed her drawings of cattle-processing plants and listened to her descriptions of the cattle procedures she wanted to be implemented, she was able to explain how her system would result in fewer cattle deaths and a calm slaughterhouse. Temple Grandin knew instinctively that she had made her point and managed to get "her foot in the door."

I agree wholeheartedly with Temple Grandin when she says that all of us on the autism spectrum must work on all areas at once: social, sensory, academic, and career. When I encounter students and parents (as I did in San Francisco) who are just looking at the academic success of their sons or daughters as a cure-all, I confront them. I speak clearly about how students with learning differences need to practice and build skills in all areas (not just one, e.g., academics). Life skills, self-care, social abilities, and preparing for a career via volunteering and internships are essential.

Community involvement

As mentioned in Chapter 2, I know that you have been your son or daughter's sole activity director, cheerleader, and biggest fan. I know that you have prodded and coaxed your child into participating in activities at high school, at college, and in your surrounding community. And I know that you have always had your son or daughter's best interests at heart.

At college or at a CIP type of program, this will be the time for your son or daughter to start belonging to and participating in the wider community. Attending activities on campus, volunteering or interning off-campus, and finding a niche that matches his or her interests will lead to a solid career and after-college plan.

The career continuum

Community service or service learning is often a first step on the career continuum. It is a safe place to learn to practice work skills and to learn to give to others. My saying is, "Community service introduces you to yourself." At CIP, we believe students learn a lot about themselves in service to others. Volunteering or participating in service-learning activities is a good place to start to learn about who they really are and what they really enjoy doing.

Volunteering or community service learning

Finding community service or service-learning projects that fit students' interest areas will allow them to gain skills for life and work doing something they like, are passionate about, or that aligns with their career goals. This can be "anything" from volunteering at the Humane Society if pets are a special interest, helping out at a food bank or soup kitchen if your young person is interested in social issues, or helping to build a house for Habitat for Humanity. Or it might be helping out a day care center, volunteering at a community garden, or even helping to paint a mural in an inner-city elementary school. In college I did a lot of community service. One of the programs I became involved with was called the Paradise Guild.

On Saturdays a group of young men and women would pile into an old station wagon and head to the Paradise Boys Orphanage just over the state line in Pennsylvania. Every single week that we could we played games and sports with the boys who lived there. We also put on holiday parties and helped make their Christmas special. I remember one year I was nominated to be Santa Claus (even though I was a tall, skinny kid). Volunteering with the Paradise Guild allowed me to give to others and, as a bonus, to receive threefold what I gave. To this day, I can remember many lessons I personally learned from the children there, and how the giving of my time and effort was so rewarding. Here are some of the things I learned that still stay with me today.

- I learned that, even though I was earning my English B.A. degree, what I really enjoyed was working with children!

- I learned that I was liked and appreciated for myself (who I truly was) and that I had a lot to offer others (especially in this type of work environment).

- I found out that I was capable of socializing with my peers (the other students from my school who were volunteering at the home) and felt accepted by them. I actually met a young woman while volunteering and she eventually became my wife. Sharing our special interest together and enjoying giving to these boys brought us together.

For me, volunteering was a "life-changing event" and taught me humility, humanity, and the value of giving my time to others. Service learning and volunteering can be a powerful way for young adults to gain self-confidence, self-esteem, and the sense of selflessness that are necessary to be successful in work and in life. These are huge lessons for your son or daughter to learn.

Internships

The placing of CIP students in suitable internships allows for further development of the essential skills necessary for life and work. This allows our students to learn to apply the academic and social knowledge they have learned in our program, in college, or career training to the real-life workplace. As my staff talk to, evaluate, and advise our students, they begin to understand what kind of internship program will be suitable for each individual.

Janet Lawson from the Autistry Studios in California says: "We must determine what each student's work rhythm is." Once they determine what placement will work and is a good match, staff will focus on helping students understand and deal with any individual difficulties and challenges they might face during the internship experience. Providing support, advice, and, when necessary, advocacy allows an internship to be successful. At CIP, we want internships to be positive and to act as a springboard for your son or daughter to navigate toward a rewarding full- or part-time job. Internships are usually unpaid; however, the knowledge and job-readiness skills your son or daughter will glean are invaluable.

To recap, the career continuum is:

- Volunteering: This is unpaid work that provides character-building, service-learning experience, and social opportunities. The scope of this volunteer work is often based upon personal interests, social or spiritual beliefs, and hobbies.

- Internship: This is usually unpaid work (or comes with a small stipend) that complements a present skill set learned at college or in career training. Internships can lead to job offers and give students the chance to experience working in a field they might like to pursue as a career. This often results in an internship-to-work agreement for many young adults whereby they are hired after a specified unpaid internship or training period.

- Employment: This is a position obtained mainly to earn money. An example might be a bagger at a grocery store.

- Career: This is a commitment to a profession that requires continued training and learned ability. A career is paid work that offers a clear path for occupational growth. Some examples would be working as a certified nursing assistant, an IT technician, a chef, a musician, an administrative assistant, a customer service representative, etc.

The career continuum

Volunteering → Community → Internship → Internship → Employment → Career
                service   to work

The following story is a good example of turning an internship into an internship-to-work experience. It details Natalie's progression from an entry-level working experience to an internship to a paid job in a field that interests her and that might lead to a solid career.

NATALIE

Natalie was a second-year student at the Massachusetts Center. She spent one day a week during her first year volunteering at a community dinner and helping out in a food pantry at a local church. Doing this helped Natalie in so many ways. She learned some valuable pre-employment skills as well as being able to acquire "customer service" ability as she talked with the older people who attended the weekly event dinners or the less fortunate members of the community who came to the food bank. Natalie really liked meeting and greeting people, and helping them, and she thought she would be really good at customer service work.

Natalie told her CIP career coordinator that she wanted to work as a cashier at a local drug store and her coordinator was able to secure an internship for Natalie. For her initial internship assignment, Natalie was taught how to do the "store inventory" and she became responsible for it.

At CIP, a career coordinator offers students realistic career counseling and advice. This includes the fact that "once on the job or internship" our students may very well have to "start at the bottom," doing the "grunt work" to prove they are capable, and have to work hard to show they have further ability. Our students soon realize that by doing this they will gain experience, become part of a team, and earn the respect from supervisors and co-workers that will lead to building a solid foundation for advancement.

In Natalie's case, she did well during her probationary period. Because of this, her career coordinator was able to approach Natalie's manager and set up an internship-to-work agreement. Natalie would continue her internship at the store for three additional months and during that time she would be trained in the operation of the cash register. If all went well, then Natalie would be hired as a cashier. This is a good example of a successful internship. Natalie gave the employer three months of "free help," and the employer gave Natalie a chance to pursue a career that would allow her to do the customer service work she coveted. Natalie successfully completed the additional three months required by the internship-to-work agreement and was hired as a paid employee.

Success stories like Natalie's are built step by step. The career continuum path helps young adults on the autism spectrum take an approach that leads to a productive and positive outcome.

At CIP, we know that our students have not had neurotypical experiences in the work world such as paper routes, babysitting, or summer jobs during high school. Skill sets may be limited or lacking. In addition to classroom instruction that helps our students develop an understanding of basic work skills, specific individual career counseling sessions help prepare them for an internship or community service work.

By taking part in an internship program or doing community or service-learning volunteer work, we know that our students may need the help of a "job coach" during the initial adjustment period from classroom to workplace. This coach helps our young adults build upon the strengths and abilities they already have and takes into consideration each individual student's special interest area.

The career counselors and job coaches who work with our students know that special interests or knowledge of a special interest often do not translate into vocational ability. We have had many students want to become sports announcers because they have the intrinsic ability to memorize all the player statistics in a specific sport that is their "special interest." Acknowledging this ability while being realistic helps our students choose a career path that is appropriate to their skill set. Willy's story is an example of how a job coach and career counselor can help bring a dream into focus and then help make it a reality.

WILLY

Willy's dream was to become a sports announcer. His career counselor at our Long Beach Center arranged for him to take a broadcasting class at the local college he was attending. Willy did really well in the class and the experience allowed him to define his "dream" career path even further. He clearly had the passion and the drive because he mastered all of his broadcasting classwork. Encouraged by Willy's hard work and determination, his counselor arranged for him to do an internship at a public-access television station.

Because of his almost natural ability in this arena, the staff at the TV station were willing to let Willy try and produce and announce a show about a local sports team in the Long Beach area. While doing this assignment, Willy became interested in using the video-editing equipment and everyone agreed that he was very good at it.

Willy's actual broadcasting debut was not the success he thought it would be and he initially felt defeated and disappointed. Even though he had great motivation, his talent lay elsewhere. The staff at the TV station were not nearly as discouraged as Willy was. They knew talent when they saw it and they helped Willy to improve his skills in the operation of all the equipment and to see how good he was with the technical side of sports casting. With the help of his job coach and career counselor, Willy was able to shift his career goal and focus into working on the technical side of broadcasting. He found a way to pursue his "special interest," that is, his love of broadcasting, and be successful at a job he was good at and qualified for, while being able to make a living at the same time.

Islands of competency

Dr. Robert Brooks from Harvard University talks about "islands of competency." By this he means that each of us has special skills that are unique and that bring goodness to the world. At CIP, we assist, assess, and help all students uncover their special island of competency. For Willy, it was a love of sports casting. For Billy, the path was quite different.

BILLY

When I was operating three children's group homes in Las Vegas back in the 70s, I had a student named Billy. Billy had cerebral palsy. He was a very nice, kind, enthusiastic young man with normal intelligence but a lot of spasticity in walking and using his arms.

One Sunday afternoon Billy and I baked a cake together and were ready to frost it. We had set everything up when the front doorbell rang. I told Billy to wait just a minute until I returned to the kitchen and went to answer the door. I got caught up at the door in a conversation with a neighbor and was delayed for about 15 minutes.

When I returned to the kitchen, I found Billy standing by the cake. I was surprised to see that the cake was perfectly iced and decorated with beautiful swirls of frosting. Billy's cake looked just like the picture on the front of a Pillsbury® Cake box. I asked him, "How did you do that?" He responded: "My mother taught me to do this when I was little."

I would never have predicted that Billy would be capable of frosting this cake. I assumed that, if left to his own devices, Billy would have made a mess of himself and the room and the cake would "look" horrible. Was I chagrined, and what a lesson I had learned! In reality, Billy's spasticity provided just the right amount of motion for him to be able to decorate a cake. His arm movements were just enough to give him the control he needed to do it well. This story is a great example of an island of competency.

We all have them. And, as it turns out, Billy's island of competency (cake decoration) turned into a career path for him. He happened to live in a city that had many casinos (Las Vegas). Each casino had a hotel attached to it and inside each hotel was a dining room that had an "all you can eat" dining buffet. Each dining facility had an enormous kitchen attached to it that made and frosted hundreds of cakes every day. Billy was able to obtain employment doing something he loved, and that he was good at doing. He turned his island of competency into a career.

Beginning a career search

Where do young adults on the autism spectrum begin career searches? I encourage young people to evoke an image or a vision of something they are interested in or even passionate about. Then I ask them to imagine making this vision into a career. At this point CIP staff will work with them to develop their interests further through education, career training, and experience. As stated before, the volunteering or internship they do in their area of interest will translate into being able to build a career portfolio and résumé.

Our students then continue to acquire skills by seeking other training opportunities or by shadowing mentors who work in the same field. Career counselors can arrange for young adults to attend free workshops and take supportive jobs at an entry level so they can build their skills and knowledge in their area of interest. As these things happen, the portfolio becomes filled with information that will increase their chances of success. Students need to see this process as one of "self-investment."

Preparing for success…the basics

At CIP, students learn to implement and use the "tools" and "rules of society" that will help them be successful as they venture out of the classroom setting and into the working world (volunteering, internships, or paid work).

Residential advisors will help your son or daughter with a head-to-toe assessment of his or her hygiene and appearance. They will stress, with kindness and compassion, the importance of making changes (if necessary) in order to align with the requirements of a volunteer, internship, or paid work environment. This includes everything from brushing teeth to choosing appropriate attire.

We let our students know that looking good can get you only so far. Having the "right attitude" is everything as they say. Students need to learn to smile and project a positive and confident image. To those on the autism spectrum this may feel fake or manipulative. Understanding that this is commonplace behavior for those in a workplace setting, and that it is "expected" behavior by employers and colleagues, will help your son or daughter master the skills necessary to do this. Your student will need to talk about this and start to understand that it is the way of the world. People want to be around people who are happy and upbeat, not glum or morose.

Learning the hidden curriculum (as discussed in Chapter 3) about proper body language and posture while "on the job" is a necessity. One example of the hidden curriculum in the workplace might be to know if it is OK to lean on a counter when talking to another person, or is it a more formal atmosphere? Or, it might be knowing that one needs to stand up if the boss comes into the room, or even being able to ask if it is OK to eat in the office at a desk or if there is a designated space for this.

Malcolm Johnson gives the following advice in his book *Managing with Asperger Syndrome* (2005, pp.36–37). He says in a section entitled "Act in a way that is appropriate to your surroundings" that:

> I have learnt that being sensitive to, and adapting to, different environments, though not easy for me, is imperative. An important practical requirement that my experience has impressed upon me is the need to assimilate and fit in with the demands of the working environment—both physical and personal.

Whilst at the investment bank I was conscious that my style of clothing, though smart and perfectly acceptable and presentable, was out of sync with that of many of my contemporaries. The need to "fit in" in this way was something that I never considered important or appreciated very deeply due to my individualism and the lack of importance that I attached to the subject.

However, style of dress is important, I believe, for credibility. As a senior manager I have found that it sends a message; more pertinently, for someone with AS, failing to adapt sends an additional signal: you are different and your failure to fit in acts as a partial reinforcement of differentness and eccentricity.

I make it an objective to try and limit my insularity by keeping my "personal uniqueness" to a minimum. It is not being different per se that is the issue; but it is important to be sensitive to others around you so as not to impact negatively upon them. Whilst remaining myself, I try to accommodate the views and styles of the environment and those I work with and respect both them and the culture that presides within the organisation.

Self-motivation

Self-motivation plays a large role in successful employment. The ability to initiate and be sincere and helpful is appreciated by all employers. Young adults on the autism spectrum need to make the shift from high school, college, or career training (where they are directed with schedules and teachers constantly), to being able to work independently and with minimal supervision. They need to understand that they will be required to give a complete and full day's work for a full day's pay. These skills need teaching and reinforcing. Having your son or daughter follow the career continuum (volunteering, interning, interning to paid work) is an effective way of teaching these skills.

Executive function in the career continuum

Executive functioning skills needed to do a job well, things like being on time and following protocol, may initially seem like easy things to accomplish for students on the autism spectrum. This is because these young adults tend to interpret rules and regulations very literally. They usually do not know how to adapt a set rule or a protocol to fit a situation. Time management also can be a problem: such students might spend an inordinate amount of time completing a task too perfectly for what is wanted or needed on the job, or rush through the task and complete it less perfectly than an employer needs or wants them to.

In Frank's story (below), the lesson learned was a costly one to the employer. This story illustrates in a very factual, "hands on," concrete way how Frank learned (with the help of his career coordinator) from his mistakes "on the job."

FRANK

Frank was a student who had recently obtained a position as a clerical assistant. He was very anxious to please his new boss, and when there was a lag in work he used his own initiative to seal the envelopes for a mailing that was being completed in the office. He assumed that he was being proactive and forward thinking; however, he did this without asking his supervisor. Frank did not know that the mailing was incomplete. He had no way of knowing that it was being held up pending one more paper that needed to be inserted in the mailing before it was to be sealed and sent out. By rushing forward and sealing the envelopes, he inadvertently cost the business many hours of additional work. He thought he was being a "self-starter" but in reality he did not know enough about office protocol or how to work in a workplace setting to accomplish this.

Frank set about learning more about how his office worked, about chain of command, and that, if he had free time, asking for additional work was the route he needed to take. He learned that it was fine to be a self-starter but only if he paid attention to the tasks at hand, communicated with others, and learned how to do his job correctly. His career coordinator provided him with a list of five tasks he could work on if he ran out of work. These tasks were agreed upon and endorsed by his employer.

Job coaching

Many students need to be coached so that they can learn what Frank learned on the job (the hard way) before they enter the workplace. Knowing that excuses are not acceptable to employers and that they just want the job done on time and correctly are things that need to be pre-learned. Using the career continuum as a working model and job coaching to be successful, your son or daughter will learn working protocol. Your young adult will also learn that making mistakes is human nature, and that practicing in being accountable and taking responsibility for the mistakes are skills he or she needs to learn. Willingness to learn workplace etiquette and protocol will help your son or daughter overcome problems on the job.

Matching the individual to the sensory environment

There is another paradox that occurs with young adults on the autism spectrum. Despite all their learning differences, their preferences for the type of environments they live and work in vary greatly and this is sometimes not according to our program's or their parents' plan or planning. Some prefer urban environments and others really like the country.

Each student needs to assess and determine what type of living and working environment will suit his or her needs. CIP centers are located in many diverse areas: rural, suburban, and urban, and students and their parents can choose a location that meets their son or daughter's needs. A compatible location is also crucial when choosing a college or university, as is the size of college or university the young adult wants to attend—some students like a smaller college and others love the sheer numbers of a large city campus.

The key is to help the young people understand how their Aspie traits or learning differences will have an impact on them in the location they choose to work, live, or go to school in, and how they can use their choice to be successful.

Finding the right sensory environment in which students on the autism spectrum can work often determines how successful they will be "on the job." Some students do well in a cubicle with other workers surrounding them. Some are fine with noise filtering in and fluorescent lights shining overhead, and others need a quiet space with dim lights.

Stephen Shore (2010) talks about his experience after he graduated from college with an accounting degree. He got a job at an accounting firm. His employer agreed he could put the bicycle that he used to and from work in the furnace room. He would also use this room to change from his bike-riding clothes to his work attire. He would then go to his desk and start his workday. The overhead lights bothered Stephen and so did the surrounding noises of his colleagues. He felt enclosed and stifled and found the work boring. After trying an "at a desk" job, he decided to study for another degree instead of staying in an environment that violated all his sensory issues.

The job Stephen had trained for, that of an accountant, was not a good fit for him even though he liked the analytical side of "doing numbers." Had he had the opportunity to do an internship in accounting at an actual accounting firm, he might have discovered this earlier.

The spaces and places that young adults work in should work for them instead of against them. If they feel comfortable in their work environment, they will be more productive and have fewer social, emotional, or work-related problems.

In some cases it may be necessary for the employer to provide an accommodation, and we encourage our students and their career counselors or parents to be open and honest about any needs regarding the workplace environment.

In most cases, employers will cooperate. If there are loud noises, bright lights, or foul smells, the employee on the autism spectrum may not be able to tolerate it and his or her anxiety level will rise. In this case, asking for an accommodation is appropriate.

Your son or daughter may be required to stand, walk, sit, or remain in one place for a long period of time, or work extraordinary hours either very early in the morning or late at night. If he or she has trouble doing this, asking for an accommodation is necessary. Can the young adult tolerate a cold, dark, or hot working site? What are his or her preferences? Are the demands of the work environment too high or anxiety producing? Are the requirements for physical exertion too much? Asking for and receiving an accommodation can make the difference between a successful or frustrating work experience.

Positives outweighing negatives

Once a workplace accommodation is made and the environment your son or daughter is in is conducive, there is much good news to be had. The positive side of Asperger's, autism, and learning differences is that many of us are always on time. We always do what we say we are going to do, and follow through on our projects. We can bring perfectionism and creative ideas to a project. We remember details that others forget. We can be put in charge of areas, and employers can rest assured that things will be done exactly the way they have asked us to do them over and over again. As Ami Klin (2010) says, "People with Asperger's may get it wrong, but they get it wrong consistently," and the same is true when we get it right!

Most studies show that intelligence is not the most important attribute in being successful at a job (although many on the autism spectrum have high IQs); perseverance and endurance are much more important and most "Aspies" sure have a lot of that.

Creating a partnership

As mentioned in Natalie's story, one of the most important concepts those on the autism spectrum need to accept is that they may have to start volunteering, doing internships, or acquiring jobs that are at an entry level. Many times this is the price of entry into a career that the young adult *really* wants. For students with learning differences, this means allowing others to have an opinion that may be different from their own. This can be very difficult for students with Asperger's, autism, or learning differences.

We had a student several years ago who would not eat in the employee cafeteria because it served Pepsi and he believed in Coke! Our students quickly find out that the world is a harsh place to be or live in if they are trying to make it conform to their own needs and opinions all the time. This is why learning to work in groups, or teams, and learning to listen and value what others are saying, is so important.

Working together as a team is a skill that needs to be taught. At CIP, career counselors, job coaches, advisors, mentors, instructors, and employers talk about the benefits of being able to be a team member and how this helps our students when they are "on the job."

Matching a student to the right employer who can understand and work with the student's particular strengths, and also on areas that need to be improved, is a science. A deeper level is then training a student to look for the type of employer he or she can feel supported by.

Flexibility while working with others, compromising, and negotiating are also skills that can be learned, and they are so important for those of us on the autism spectrum. As an "Aspie" dad who has raised four teenage daughters, I can say with authority that there is an art to learning to negotiate, especially with young adults! You have to be willing to compromise (very hard for an "Aspie" dad to do). When my daughters reached the point where they wanted to stay overnight at friends' houses (sometimes on a school night, which was against my house rules), we had a chance to learn negotiation and compromise skills. As inflexible as I was,

I somehow knew these were opportunities to teach valuable skills and I took advantage of them. I did not have the awareness or presence of mind always to be able to do this, but, when I could, I was glad I did.

Asking for help, directions, or advice

Students need to develop the navigation skills necessary to be able to make it out in the employment world. This not only applies to being able to navigate the workplace and social environments but physical and directional navigation as well. The primary rule we teach our students when encountering any of these roadblocks is to "gather up their courage and ask for help!" We tell them that they can get answers, obtain solutions, and even physically find their way anywhere if they are willing to ask for help, advice, or directions.

Last spring I got off an airplane in Sydney, Australia, and got into my rental car. I had to contend with driving on the left side of the road *and* following my MapQuest directions to my hotel in Newtown at the same time. I realized almost immediately that the directions were wrong. No matter how hard I looked I could not find the road I needed. I was on an interstate highway heading toward a tunnel and I had to make myself accept the fact that I was going to get off the first exit after the tunnel and stop and ask directions again. I know following driving directions is not a strength I possess so, in preparation for this trip, I had (on the QT) given myself permission to screw up the directions part of the trip. While giving myself this permission, I took the time and established a couple of rules for myself. When driving in Australia:

1. I would take my time and not be rushed into any turns or any driving decisions. I would simply pull over if I had a problem and not allow physical distress or stress to take over.

2. I would always just stay left on any road I ended up on. In fact, I made two labels to stick on the steering wheel and dashboard that said "STAY LEFT" on them.

I also arranged for my flight to arrive early in the day so I could drive in daylight and take my time to find my way. I had to stop three times to get directions and in the end I got where I needed to go with as little physical and emotional distress as possible.

The techniques I use each day to navigate my job, organize my life, and regulate my emotions were learned through trial and error. I did a lot of reading, self-education, and experimentation to find systems and ways to make myself successful in my career and in interpersonal and even casual relationships.

CIP has taken the best of what works for me, and what we know from experience works for our students as they navigate leaving high school or college and venturing out into the world of work. The career continuum process we have created at our centers offers young adults a head start on figuring out how to obtain work that is meaningful and rewarding, and gives them the experience through volunteering and internships to learn techniques described in this chapter. And…if they are ever heading to Australia, I have that system down pat and would be glad to pass that on too!

Chapter 8

Handling Finances

Money Makes the World Go Round

Thank you for all You have given me. Help me to be unselfish, do the right thing, and be honest and loving in all my dealings.

Most young people have had some experience with managing their own money. However, when they go off to school or leave home for a job and then move into their own apartment, it may be the first time that they are handling money on a daily basis. Before financial independence can happen, parents need to sit down with their sons and daughters before they go off to school, help them make a budget, and give good, solid advice about daily money management.

Being able to handle money is necessary. In order for students to become self-reliant with day-to-day expenses and to have the self-confidence necessary to make appropriate money decisions, they need to understand the role that money plays. This chapter explains how staff at CIP teach students on the autism spectrum to budget, manage money, and retain funds. Being fiscally aware takes young adults on a path that leads to making wise financial decisions, and that in turn leads to real-life skills for living independently and managing money responsibly.

CIP's money management programs are proactive. The examples we portray and the advice we impart imitate real-life situations. We strive to create an atmosphere of success and accomplishment because we advise each young adult individually. The classroom examples show our students how to respond to the daily challenges of handling their own funds. It also illustrates that these skills are teachable.

There seems to be an ATM machine on every corner. College students in general, as well as those on the autism spectrum, often have difficulty being accountable for their money. The easy access to cash that ATMs provide means that money is available 24 hours a day. Some students, when faced with a financial problem, will say, "It's alright, I will just go to the ATM machine!" For students with Asperger's, autism, or learning differences, this situation will be exacerbated by financial naïveté. Will Rogers famously said: "The quickest way to double your money is to fold it and put it back in your wallet."

At CIP, we show students that something as simple as taking out a fixed amount of money at the beginning of each week, and allotting that money wisely until the following weekly withdrawal, allows them to use the ATM with discretion.

By learning to budget, our young students learn to be realistic about meeting their daily needs and expenses in a proactive way. The traits that accompany Asperger's, autism, and learning differences, and lead to repetitive and rigid thought patterns that are often counterproductive, surface when it comes to money management. The challenge is teaching young adults to become flexible and open to mastering the skills needed for learning to handle money.

My own experience—related below—has served me well and is useful as a key point when I speak publicly. For instance, I recently renovated an historic building in Lee, Massachusetts (a $3.7 million project), using my past history of paying bills on time and paying off mortgages, and using the financial savvy that was gleaned from an early age of learning how to handle and master money, as the kingpin for the project. Years and years of being penny wise and never pound foolish paid off—the CIP Berkshire Center has a state-of-the-art facility with attached art gallery and organic café and is the showpiece of Main Street, Lee.

MICHAEL'S EXPERIENCE

When I was in junior high school, my mom helped me get a paper route. She explained that "all" my brothers had paper routes at my age (12) and that I was expected to have one too. She explained that it would teach me the value of a good work ethic and allow me to earn some money. As part of the deal, I was to pay for the family's daily paper out of the money I earned *and* contribute some of my money toward the family expenses. With seven brothers and sisters going to private schools and colleges, it was clear that I was expected to do my share.

I learned to save my money for things I really wanted and, being the undiagnosed little "Aspie" that I was, I always had a nice balance in my bank account. My sisters would try to manipulate me into buying them expensive presents or giving them money, but I instinctively knew that my money was my money and I guarded it!

I always say that one day I went away to college in Maryland and four years later my parents picked me up. My dad paid my tuition and my room and board. I was responsible for books, travel, and spending money. When I wanted a car, I saved my money and bought one. The rigidity and inflexibility of my then undiagnosed Asperger's Syndrome set the scene for me to become a good money manager.

I only made this connection and realized the effect having Asperger's had on my early money management abilities about a year ago. The "Aspie" traits that I had grown up with, and my family's insistence that I work and be responsible for helping our family out, helped me build a foundation for financial success. I can honestly say that I have never missed a payroll payment to my staff in the 28 years that I have operated CIP centers. I never took out a business loan (I remembered the advice my dad gave me: try not to borrow money but, if you do, try not to pay any interest!) or borrowed against the company's assets.

When parents put this type of money management philosophy and ideas into an Aspie's brain, *we* take them literally. Teaching young adults on the autism spectrum to manage money is usually very effective. At CIP, we have found our students also get the technical side of balancing a checkbook, using software like Finance Works or QuickBooks, and obtain a genuine sense of mastery and competence in knowing where every penny goes and where every penny is.

Parents weigh in

Several years ago, I asked parents whose students had recently graduated from our Berkshire Center what they thought we, at CIP, could do better. One parent said: "Make them struggle more to prepare for the real world they are facing after leaving the program." She then followed this statement by saying: "Give them less spending money so that they learn to live on less, learn to budget their money more tightly, and *then* increase the challenges they will have to overcome as they move through the process." I took this to heart. When you think about it, this is what every good teacher does, and teaching young adults about money should follow this same process. I wholeheartedly challenge all parents reading this book to start teaching money management skills to your young adults, *today*, while they are still at home.

Being generous and being careful

At CIP, we know that our students sometimes try to win friends and influence others by giving gifts or buying them things that they cannot afford. We also know that they can be vulnerable when being asked to lend others money. It is easy for those on the autism spectrum to misread a situation or a social cue.

In Chapter 5, I talked about a young man named Jeff who bought expensive boxes of Valentine candy for two young women he barely knew. Sometimes, students who have not mastered social thinking competencies are so desperate for a relationship or a friendship that they will use money inappropriately.

This also happened in the story I relayed about Mark and his manipulative friend Josh. Knowing that our students can be easily coerced into giving or lending money to others sets the scene for CIP staff to work on making students aware of these pitfalls. We offer, teach, and give students strategies and solutions for these tricky situations. We do this via role-playing, instruction in money management, and one-on-one help in areas that need strengthening.

Learning strategies and techniques, and practicing areas that need reinforcing, as well as becoming financially grounded, help young adults take one further step toward being able to live responsibly and independently.

Financing special interests

Another common problem we deal with on a daily basis is that our students will often become obsessed with buying things that are related to their area of special interest. Parents can unwittingly reinforce this behavior. After all, what parent doesn't want to encourage their son or daughter's interest by allowing him or her to make purchases in order to do so? Especially when the special interest the money goes toward makes their son or daughter so happy.

Other financial difficulties occur when students are not able to utilize common sense. Because of the way Asperger's, autism, and learning differences work, using common sense is an abstract concept to some of our students and one that is difficult to understand. When this failure occurs, we usually find that our students have fed their special interests by buying things that are beyond their spending means.

More often though, we see the opposite occur—students who follow the rules and save all their money and refuse to spend any of it on themselves. We have had students who will wear the same clothes until they fall apart. They might forego activities with classmates, or stay home when others are eating out, because they do not want to spend any money. Some students go to an extreme and hoard money.

Remember how literal an "Aspie" can be. In taking financial responsibility to heart, parents may have told their sons or daughters that they need to be especially "good at handling their money," so their young adults take this to an extreme. There are saving extremes and spending extremes. Chris's story illustrates how he conquered spending nearly all of his allotted money on his particular area of special interest.

CHRIS

Chris was a CIP student from Toronto, Canada, who was obsessed with "video gaming." He owned the latest version of every video game and game player on the market. He was so involved in his special interest that he monitored websites for new releases and would purchase these products the minute they hit the market. He had several bookcases filled with his prized possessions.

This behavior in a 14-year-old would be understandable. Parents would monitor a child of this age and set limits on spending. Chris's problem was that he was 22 years old, attending CIP, and trying to master the skills necessary for independent living, including money management.

CIP staff and Chris's parents knew that he used gaming and the purchasing of gaming materials as substitutes to avoid moving forward in the academic, career, and social areas of his life. Staff also knew that Chris would need to acknowledge this and then be willing to look at alternatives and to take offered suggestions to curb his behavior.

When approached by staff, Chris was initially unwilling to put gaming into balance with the other areas of his life. When we talked to his parents, they let us know that they wanted to support him in what seemed to be the one and only area of his life that he enjoyed. Their view was that, if you took gaming away from him, he would not have anything left in his life. This was not our intention. We were looking to help him achieve a balance that would put his finances in order, allow for gaming, and also open up opportunities to move in new directions.

Achieving this balance with Chris took some time. He worked with his therapist, his advisor, and CIP's career coordinator to come up with a compromise that he, his parents, and the rest of the CIP staff would approve. With input from CIP staff, Chris's parents put a limit on his spending. He knew that he could not make a new purchase until all his monthly bills were paid. Having this new structure allowed him the time to work on other areas of his life. In time, he gained the emotional balance needed to start socializing with others. Once he did this, other interest areas came into his life. He started forging friendships with his peers (some were interested in "gaming" and others were outside the "gaming world").

This was a delicate, well-planned process for the CIP staff members who were involved. They did not want to become surrogate parents and Chris's parents did not want to seem punitive or controlling. It was important for Chris to see for himself that he needed to make changes, and then he had to want to change. With compassion and full staff support, Chris was able to align his spending and his special interest with making friends and, to his surprise, he discovered he was interested in hiking, skateboarding, and going out on Saturday nights for a movie and a pizza.

Credit cards

Another tricky area is deciding if your son or daughter will have or be able to use credit cards. We ask parents to place limits on any credit cards their young adults bring to a CIP residential program. For example, when my son moved out of a dorm and decided to share an apartment with friends, I gave him a credit card with a $500 a month limit on it. Within this limit, he had to budget for food, clothes, and all social activities. It took him a while to be able to stay within his monthly budget but the structure I put in place helped him understand and put limits on his spending.

We also talk about how important it is to ignore and not respond to any credit card offers that appear in campus mailboxes. Credit card companies target students and we know that our students are especially vulnerable. We teach them credit card hygiene too: this means not lending credit cards to roommates or friends, shredding credit card statements that have their credit card numbers on them, and being vigilant about where a card is (i.e., in a wallet, desk, or backpack) at all times.

Starting off on the right foot

Being proactive with students and allowing them to experience money management success sets the stage for financial independence from parents. At CIP, we know that our students want this responsibility and usually respond positively to the challenge of handling their own finances. As they become flexible and open to our teaching, they learn to budget, pay monthly bills, and plan for purchases and unseen or unexpected expenses.

Before your son or daughter goes off to school, see if he or she can take responsibility for paying for clothes, food, or nights out with friends on a fairly regular basis. If your son or daughter has a credit card, discuss how placing limits will work for all of you. Do not wait to have that conversation until your young adult has overspent or let the card reach its credit limit.

Chapter 9

Feeling Fit, Groomed, and Fueled

Health and Wellness

Happiness comes from within you: what you eat and how you take care of yourself determine how you show up in life and in the world.

THREE YEARS AND SIX MONTHS

— MY HAPPINESS IS WITHIN ME

— I CAN CHANGE NO ONE ELSE

— I CAN CHOOSE TO BE HAPPY EACHDAY

— BEING IN ME IN A LOVING WAY
     GOES OUT TO OTHERS

— TRUE ACCEPTANCE OF MY REAL FEELINGS
     LETS ME BE FREE

— I AM WORTHY ALREADY

— THERE IS NOTHING I HAVE TO DO OR HAVE
     TO BE HAPPY

— I ALREADY HAVE EVERYTHING I NEED

— EVERYTHING IS A BONUS

— I SURRENDER, I ACCEPT, I AM
     GRATEFUL AND I WANT TO BE COMPASSIONATE

— I WAS MADE FOR GOOD PURPOSE AND I
     AM INHERENTLY VALUABLE

— MY HAPPINESS IS WITHIN ME

6/13/07

I have learned the hard way how maintaining a healthy lifestyle can help those of us on the autism spectrum reduce stress and elevate levels of functioning. Exercise and good diet increase energy, promote positive social behaviors, and strengthen our immune systems. A healthy lifestyle also helps us improve our self-esteem and how we perceive and view others.

Students on the spectrum need to figure out what type of diet, exercise, or activity will work best for them. After an individual assessment, CIP students can then focus on the specific areas of nutrition, hygiene, sensory diets, weight control, and physical fitness that will serve them best. As with so many things in this book, awareness is the first step to understanding what will work best for your son or daughter. This awareness then becomes the motivator that leads to making healthy changes and incorporating new behaviors.

Students on the spectrum face unique challenges and hurdles as they develop and try to maintain a healthy lifestyle. I will often talk to students and staff members about the strategies they use to promote good health. I also share ways that have worked for me, and illustrate how the little changes I am constantly making often make a big difference in the way I feel.

Unfortunately or fortunately, the habits we form as children often predict how we take care of ourselves as adults. In my case, my family didn't engage in physical activities or exercise very often. They mostly sat around, ate high-calorie snacks and sodas, and watched television. I mirrored this.

Things changed a bit in the summertime. We belonged to an outdoor swim club and I loved being outside and "in the pool." I swam the backstroke competitively and, in one of those small ironies in life, my female counterpart on the swim team was none other than the famous Susan Sarandon (formerly little Suzie Tomlin of Edison, New Jersey). My 15 minutes of fame aside, swimming is still one of my favorite ways to get exercise and decrease stress. I do this as often as I can. When I start to swim, it is as though I am hitting the reset button on my computer screen and righting all that has been wrong that day. As I immerse myself in water, stress dissipates and it feels like the internal core of my nuclear power plant is cooling off. When I was younger, I envisioned steam coming out of my ears.

A few years ago I began to seriously take care of myself: I closely watch what I eat, how much I sleep, how much exercise I get, what I do to maintain my sensory diet, and, above all, I now get a yearly physical exam. This has made a big difference in how I handle my Asperger's Syndrome.

Balancing nutrition, sleep, and exercise

At college or a program like mine, your young adult should work with the wellness department or center to design a plan that especially takes into consideration his or her specific challenges and needs. This might be working on a more nutritious way of eating, weight management, or maintaining a sensory diet or nightly sleep routine.

I know from being one once that college-age students tend to abuse their bodies. They stay up all hours and can live on potato chips and sodas. In fact, being away from home for the first time provides young adults with the independence to do exactly as they please. This is no different for young adults with Asperger's, autism, or learning differences. However, those on the spectrum tend to do exactly as they please while staying in their rooms for days at a time (isolating), completely losing track of time, and/or not getting enough sleep.

At CIP we teach our students that the food they eat and the amount of sleep they get nightly, as well as the exercise they choose to engage in, may seem boring or repetitive but that is OK and just fine for now. The important thing is that they are making positive choices and decisions about their lives and their bodies. We teach nutrition, how to grocery shop, and that eating a variety of foods and mixing in some vegetables and fruit along with good proteins will help students stay alert and keep their weight in check.

We also advocate looking and feeling good through good grooming habits. Your young adult will learn that the basics include a daily shower and a change of clothes; otherwise a roommate may be offended by the odor not doing these things will cause. An accumulation of dirty laundry will also cause problems. In addition to the smell that might start to emanate from sweaty, damp, or wet clothes and towels being left on the floor or in a laundry basket, mold, mildew, and imbedded dirt may ruin the clothes or never wash out.

Sensory issues

In our program, we work to make sensory issues tolerable. Sounds, light, touch, feel, smell, audio, and visual issues will usually surface very early in the life of a child with Asperger's, autism, or a learning difference. Tolerance levels for these sensory issues vary. Some students on the autism spectrum who suffer from sensory overload can barely get through Thanksgiving dinner without creating a family rift that will last for years. Others need to wash clothing until it is super soft; still others wear a baseball cap with a large bill to deflect fluorescent lighting, or use white noise to block out sounds.

Your son or daughter will need to develop personal pro-social coping mechanisms for dealing with the individual sensory onslaught that he or she is experiencing. I have had students wear the same clothing repeatedly because it is comfortable, and some who will only wear certain colors of clothing. Many need to cut the labels out of clothing, because these are offensive and bothersome. Some of our students will alter their entire daily routine to avoid certain sensory stimuli: noises, smells, or overhead lighting.

In order to wear a dress shirt and tie, I need to purchase shirts with wide collars and then tie my tie loosely so I don't feel like I am choking. A couple of years ago I decided to be the "guinea pig" to test out the neuro-feedback system a doctor was using with a few students at our Florida program. I had him hook me up to equipment and I practiced keeping two lines near each other on a monitor.

I had 16 sessions over a couple of months. The doctor used this analogy to describe what was going on in my brain. He said:

> Michael, it's like every time you want to go to Orlando, you have to create new directions and take a different set

of side streets to get there. It is a tremendous amount of work and you expend an enormous amount of energy figuring it out each time. But you are very creative and work hard to do it.

I am going to put you on the super highway. You will be able to take the interstate much faster and use much less mental energy.

One of our parents recently wrote a story about her son Steve's sensory journey and sent it to me for inclusion in this book. It illustrates several of the key points that I am trying to make.

STEVE

Steve's mother writes:

My son Steve graduated from high school truly by the skin of his teeth. Although he was an honors student and varsity track athlete, the last two years of attending a large public school became increasingly challenging for him because of his many sensory issues. During Steve's junior year, when students typically begin looking forward to the transition from home to college life, he felt overwhelmed and anxious. Diagnosed with Asperger's at age 12, his sensory issues started to surface more significantly as he began his journey to adulthood.

Students who accidentally elbowed Steve in the crowded corridors at school began to make him feel extremely uncomfortable. When a metal desk scraped against the hard classroom floor, the sound this made was almost too much for him to bear. The pressure from coaches on his track team to be a top finisher at county meets became increasingly stressful. High-pitched noises such as fire sirens became so loud for him that he began to wear noise-cancelling headphones in public places. Steve's overloaded senses and anxiety levels escalated so dramatically during his last year of high that he stopped attending classes. He struggled to finish his remaining course work through the school district's independent study program.

After receiving his high school diploma, Steve decided he was not interested in pursuing an education or a career. He spent more and more time alone in his room, either playing video games or sitting on his bed in the dark. Concerned with his downward spiral, Steve's dad and I researched post-high school options for young adults with Asperger's and learning differences. We found two programs that looked like they might be a good fit. We then asked him to consider both schools and told him that being isolated in his room was no longer an option.

Steve agreed to visit the two post-high school programs. He was somewhat interested in CIP (the College Internship Program) because it was close to his hometown and this town was in his comfort zone. While he was not motivated to attend college or do much of anything, Steve did agree to attend CIP.

In the beginning, his progress was slow. He spent a great deal of time in his apartment by himself. When he ventured out, he wore a baseball hat that he pulled down around his eyes. He never made eye contact with anyone. Our Steve was, however, a rule follower. He attended all of the required classes that were scheduled for him at CIP including the classes that taught him how he might cope with some of his sensory issues. This paid off. The classes gave him a framework for tackling each sensory issue one step at a time. He learned that he needed to ask for accommodations in classroom settings and to be able to wear a baseball cap with a large bill and to sit close to a door so that he could quietly leave without drawing attention to himself if he was in distress or suffering an anxiety attack.

Gradually, Steve began to gain interest in continuing his education. He had been deeply concerned about global warming and deforestation since childhood, so the earth sciences intrigued him. With the help and encouragement from his advisor, Steve enrolled in a geology class at a local community college. With the continued support of his advisor and tutor, he began to embrace the curriculum and finished the semester with an A in the class. Steve also began participating in organized social events and occasionally exchanged pleasantries with others.

After attending CIP, Steve decided he was ready to enroll in a four-year university and study geology. Although he still struggles to meet new people and make friends, he is living independently at college and made the President's honor roll recently with a 4 grade point average. Steve hopes to graduate from college and find meaningful work helping to reforest the earth.

I can relate to Steve. In the story "Young Michael," my own fears and ways of coping emerge as I struggle to find some semblance of calm and quiet and the so-important "accommodations" I devised to help me help myself.

Young Michael

As a child, I was afraid of loud noises and I would cry when I heard a siren. I ate only peanut butter or butter sandwiches for lunch throughout elementary school. I would not eat any fruit and very few vegetables (a texture thing). I hated holidays because my entire family would be there with other relatives and family friends, and the house would be full of people, noise, and a changed schedule. I was often sensorially overwhelmed throughout childhood.

Growing up as an "Aspie" and one of the youngest in a family of smokers was a sensory nightmare. Like Steve in the last story, I was a rule follower. In a family where my sisters and brothers slept in until noon on weekends, I was always up early. On Sundays, my family always went to church. Because of all the late sleepers, we would inevitably arrive at the church late.

This meant we had to stand at the back of the church because there were no seats left. These were all major rule violations in my book and caused me much distress. The priest would always remark about those standing along the side of the pews and I felt he was talking personally to me.

On the way to and from the church I would be squished into our big old car as everyone lit up cigarettes and talked loudly. Between our being late, and the cigarette smoking, I was a bundle of anxiety every Sunday. At this young age, I figured out a way to cope. I would get up early and walk a few miles, and attend the early mass by myself.

This is how I learned to start making accommodations for my sensory issues. Not ideal of course, but my strategies worked. The walk provided me with peace and quiet. And, as an added bonus, getting up when the rest of the family was still sleeping allowed me to have silence and calm as I prepared for church— it was a double win. I also had the house to myself when they were in church!

As a young adult, no one told me that I would have sensory issues when it came to being in a relationship. I just thought I was just like anyone else. I soon realized that I didn't like to be touched in certain ways or for a certain amount of time. I didn't realize how much the sense of smell mattered when I lived with someone else. I didn't realize how sensitive I would be to daily living sounds, fabrics on furniture, and an overall household environment.

I had a lot of difficulty sharing my space with another person. As a freshman in college, I had a roommate who liked to go out at night and come in late, and he made noise when he came in. He was also messy and I could not handle all his stuff being left around the room. My solution was to put a physical line down the middle of the room. I then told him to keep everything on his side of the room. I never explained that his messiness bothered me or asked him if he could come in more quietly. Since I did not know I had sensory issues, I could not tell him about them.

My roommate was engaging in normal college behavior (I was the one who had the odd schedule and was overly sensitive). I, however, felt that he was doing this on purpose and he became the enemy to me. He was violating the rules and I was keeping them. I know now that I was not a good communicator, so I just internalized it. Things got so bad one evening that everything I had bottled up came out.

That ended our relationship, and he never returned to the room. Of course, I know now that issues with roommates and lifestyles need to be dealt with daily and, had I known about or had more knowledge about my own sensory issues, things might have turned out differently.

The world of girls and having a girlfriend was sensorially challenging as well. I could not stand being close to their hair and faces; the smells from the hairspray and cosmetics they used bothered me. I preferred to be with a young woman dressed in casual clothing, who did not wear make-up or perfume. This was the opposite of what the girls I wanted to be around liked—for a date or an event out came all my sensory violators. To say the least, I did not have an easy time being around females or dating.

Creating sensory comfort

Young adults need to choose clothing that makes them feel comfortable and secure. For me, it had to do mostly with the softness of the fabric and the feel of the garment against my skin. For your son or daughter it may be wearing things that are loose or flowing. Adjusting lighting so that nothing glares, or soundproofing the room where he or she sleeps, are also ways to gain sensory relief.

At CIP, we approach handling sensory issues by doing a sensory profile. We believe that wellness and sensory integration work together.

Once your son or daughter develops a wellness plan, sensory diet, and sleep diet, he or she will have the tools to customize these to fit his or her lifestyle. For instance, in my case, I fly a lot for my job, speaking internationally, and I am often traveling or preparing to travel. In order to survive the "sensory assault" of being in an airport and then on a plane, I have had to come up with a "sensory plan" to maintain my sanity.

A sensory plan for airports

Airports and airplanes are difficult places for some of us on the autism spectrum to exist in. Just the sounds alone: carts beeping; loud, garbled announcements over intercoms; people talking loudly on their cell phones; televisions blaring; children crying or playing loudly; people bumping into you with their baggage; the security searches; poor food; and I could go on and on. To help myself (and I happily pass this on to others), I came up with a sensory diet that works for me when flying and traveling:

- I wear soft clothing and bring a warm zipping-hooded sweatshirt or sweater (I can put it on if it is cold and pull it over my head if I am resting and don't want to be disturbed; it also serves as an extra pillow). I don't wear a belt. I wear shoes that you can slip on and off at security and to aid in comfort on the flight. I wear warm socks so my feet are cozy.

- Depending on what airline I am on, I make sure that I get in the first boarding group and select a window seat. I scan for little children and sit as far away from them as possible. I love kids dearly, but not on airplanes and not for hours at a time.

- If I am changing time zones, two days before the flight I wake up or go to bed earlier depending on which direction I am going. I try to half-adjust to the time change in two segments, so that it is not such a shock to my system.

- I make sure I do some meditation, prayer, and yoga before leaving for the airport no matter where I am or what city I am in. Airport interdenominational chapels are usually empty and a great place to meditate or stretch out. When I am at home, this is my usual routine, and I do not vary this even if I am doing yoga on the floor of a Holiday Inn.

- I drink a lot of water the day before the flight and the morning of the flight, because I now know what happens when my body gets dehydrated. And not drinking enough water makes my jetlag worse.

- I pack most of my own food and healthy snacks and fruit.

- I don't sit down until I get on the flight and most times I will take at least a half-hour walk around the airport after checking in.

- If I am particularly anxious or wound up, I will find an unused gate and stretch out or do push-ups to get some sensory relief.

- When standing in line for a long time, I massage my hands and arms, stand up and down on my toes, flex my legs, or push one hand against the other.

- I do my itinerary homework and use the computer to find out where I will be flying and what route the plane will take. When I board the plane, I locate myself on the side of the plane that is going to go over the best scenery (e.g., if I am flying from Oakland to Nashville and I am on the right side of the plane, I will see Yosemite National Park out the window and maybe the Grand Canyon coming out of Las Vegas).

- If the airline has open seating (I fly Southwest Airlines and they do not assign seats—it is first come, first served), I find out how many people will be on the flight. If it is full, I look for a front window seat. If there are seats free, I go to the second-to-last aisle (the last aisle's seats don't push back) and choose the window seat.

- I don't eat or drink anything served on planes if I can help it, especially pretzels, chips, and sodas.

- I time my bathroom breaks to be in the middle of the flight and then do some stretching in the back of the plane for 15 or 20 minutes.

After all, it is really about the weather inside you, rather than the weather outside the plane. I used to be tossed about by the weather conditions and, even though I cannot always totally predict the forecast, I have "Doppler radar" when I use my sensory diet. My early warning detection systems are operating and I can take steps and prevent the storm or, if need be, evacuate! When the clouds start coming in, unlike the weatherman, I can produce blue skies.

I have learned to ask for what I need and our students and staff do this as well. One of our students was preparing for a flight home from our Brevard, Florida, Center to Philadelphia. He worked with his social mentor to prepare for the flight. The student was anxious and knew that he would need a variety of IT devices to accompany him through security so that he could cope with the long flight. The center's Director called the airport and explained that the mentor would need to accompany the student through security and stay with him until he had actually boarded the plane.

This accommodation was made by the airport staff and the airline was contacted as well; neither could have been more helpful to our young adult. When he and his mentor arrived at the airport, the mentor checked in with the head of security, he notified the screeners, and our student went effortlessly through the screening process with his mentor.

The TSA staff were prepared to see a backpack that contained several computer-gaming devices, an iPod, a computer, an iPad, two cell phones, and various other things (all of an electronic nature). Our student was treated with dignity and respect and was able to have a successful flight.

We come to wellness and healthy lifestyles through various challenges and experiences. The advice given here, and the "wellness plan form" provided at the end of the chapter, are a good starting point for people on the autism spectrum who are making choices that will help them cope with their individual differences. I took the basic advice and then developed my own unique way of handling travel and airports. Your son or daughter, too, can develop a variety of coping mechanisms through trial and error.

As a small child, I did not know that I had Asperger's Syndrome but I found a way to cope with internal distress. It is my hope that your young adult will use the techniques, tips, and methodology outlined here to lessen stress and distress, and lead a happy and meaningful life.

Using prayer, meditation, and yoga—Michael speaks from the heart

I have always prayed at night growing up, and of course in Catholic schools we learned all the standard prayers by heart (or should I say rote?). My heart entered into it but not on a personal and deep level. It was not until I was in Al-Anon and AA for nine years that I dared ask myself the question: What is God to me? The answer came swiftly in visualization. In my mind I saw big block letters across the sky spelling the word "UNCONDITIONAL." At that moment, I felt that God loved me unconditionally, exactly as I was, and that I was made for good purpose.

The 11th step of AA and Al-Anon says, "Sought through prayer and meditation to improve our conscious contact with God, as we understood Him, praying ONLY for knowledge of His will for us and the power to carry that out." I had always prayed the best way I could, but never really did meditation as an ongoing practice.

About five years ago, I started to meditate for short times in the morning. I combined this with stretching and some yoga positions. I noticed that my meditation tended to stay with me many times throughout the day and I was able to be serene and calmer than I used to be. Many times my distracted mind would relax enough, and out of the fog and mist would arise a solution to a troubling problem that I would never have thought of. My mind seemed clearer and balanced.

I am a morning person and really enjoy my quiet time in the morning. I open the French doors on the third story of my house overlooking my garden, coy pond, and the forest. I listen to the birds and just let it all pass by me as the sun rises in the East. I have been able to do my practice in hotel rooms throughout the world and even standing in a crowded airport. It has brought me peace and, when I stray from my practice, I start to feel anguish, anxiety, and defensiveness come in. When I am doing my practice, I feel joy, ease, lightness, and a lack of worry and fear.

Wellness plan form

Here is the wellness plan form we use at CIP.

College Internship Program
Wellness Program
Personal Fitness Contract

1. Individual and group assessments
2. First 6-week goals achieved/reviewed
3. Second 6-week goals achieved/reviewed
4. Introduction to nutrition and diet plans

My fitness partner is: . . . .

This is the person who will help you throughout the first half of the year. Turn to the person sitting next to you, or if you already have someone in mind in the room you can ask them.

Signature of fitness partner: . . . .

Mobile #: . . . .

My weekly reminder will be put here: . . . .

Write down a specific place in your apartment where you can hang your weekly schedule. Exercises are added to your weekly schedule during your individual meeting or during your group meeting and should be performed on the day they are assigned.

Circle one:

Have you participated in team sports before?

Y or N

Have you participated in individual sports before?

Y or N

Do you have severe medical factors hindering certain exercises?

Y or N

*Remember: if you miss your workout on the day you're supposed to complete it, make it up the next day or as soon as possible. Missing one or two days does not mean the whole week was unsuccessful, but it means you need to reschedule and use time management skills in order to be successful! Twenty minutes of physical activity will make you feel better both physically and mentally!

Your signature: . . . .

Date: . . . .

Wellness coordinator's signature: . . . .

Date: . . . .

My exercise goals

These are exercises that are achievable but still difficult. Think of something you currently cannot do and write it down! Think of short-term and long-term goals. Easier goals should be considered short term and can be written in the 1 month column. Harder goals should be written in the 3 month or 6 month column. List three goals for each month.

My personal goals

Here is a list of goals one might set for themselves for the next six months. Setting long-term goals and reviewing their success/reasons for failure at short increments allows someone the opportunity to revise their goals and find different, more effective ways of acquiring them.

*Remember the A,B,C,Ds! Your goals should be:

1. Attainable and appropriate—if you've never run before, don't plan to run a marathon two months from now.

2. Beneficial: applied to other areas of improvement, i.e., Exec. Functioning.

3. Clearly written—rather than resolving to "get buff," aim to accomplish a specific goal by a certain date—like being able to run 3 miles or consistently exercise with your fitness partner.

4. Directly in view every day.

Example goals:

- Keep weekly schedule in convenient place and arrive on time to all appointments.

- Be consistent in my sleep patterns to stay alert and healthy.

- Have a greater awareness of how my schedule affects overall wellness.

- Resolve personal conflicts appropriately and in a timely manner.

- Take prescriptions consistently and on time.

- Eat less processed foods and sodas; READ the nutrition labels.

- Develop stronger positive relationships with those around me.

- Exercise 3–4 times a week and maintain a regular exercise schedule.

Write your personal goals below:

(Remember to prioritize by 1. Easily Attainable to 5. Difficulty Attaining)

1. . . . .

2. . . . .

3. . . . .

4. . . . .

5. . . . .

6. . . . .

Example goals table

Goals	Weeks					
	WEEK 1	WEEK 2	WEEK 3	WEEK 4	WEEK 5	WEEK 6
First goal is easiest to accomplish Awareness of How Scheduling Affects Health	➤					
Keep Weekly Schedule in Convenient Place and Be On Time		➤				
Take Meds Consistently and On Time			➤			
Resolve Personal Conflicts Appropriately and Timely				➤		
Be Consistent in Sleep Patterns					➤	
Eat Less Junk Food Last goal is most difficult to accomplish						➤

Goals	Week 1	Week 2	Week 3	Week 4	Week 5	Week 6
1						
2						
3						
4						
5						
6						

Months			
I month	3 months	6 months	I year

Notes:

Learning the "Hidden Curriculum"

Friendship then Love

We must forge ourselves into what we want, hope for, and can't live without. Risking to love—over and over again. Putting ourselves back on the track over and over again.

Young adults on the autism spectrum need to explore their own individual attitudes and values regarding healthy relationship development. They need to embrace who they truly are and learn to accept this, especially when it comes to forming friendships and dating. At CIP, this is done in a helpful and compassionate way through Relationship Development classes. It often amazes me what comes out in each class session and how this information gives staff an accurate perspective on what our students are thinking and feeling about relationships. We know from experience that many of our young adults have experienced rejection, ostracism, and bullying during their grade school, middle school, and high school years. They leave home after high school for college or a CIP type of program with those experiences very much in the forefront.

Our Relationship Development classes were created to address the issues surrounding relationships and skills for surmounting difficulties. Hidden curriculum instruction gives our young adults the ability to differentiate the norms of society from experiences that could lead to danger or trouble. Some of this class curriculum is based on the hidden curriculum work of Brenda Smith Myles, who serves on CIP's National Professional Advisory Board.

The information we give to young adults imparts practical, social, and emotional knowledge, and then gives them the strategies to form and develop friendships built around common interests. We know that all young people on the autism spectrum need to explore their own individual attitudes and values regarding healthy relationship development, and to gain a comfort level with this.

As stated in the "Dating on campus" section in Chapter 2, we advocate that students take it slowly in the beginning. This approach gives our students time to practice and then adjust socially. Encouragement to keep trying and reaching out to others is done with kindness and support.

In the general "hidden curriculum" section in Chapter 3, I talked about learning the instinctive codes that neurotypicals take for granted. Forming friendships and then deeper and meaningful relationships requires the ability to differentiate actual reality from expected or wanted reality. We teach the right ways and show the wrong ways to our students.

For instance, the right way of expressing interest in another person of the opposite sex would be to say "Hello" from a distance to see if the person is interested. If the person is, he or she will make eye contact in return, smile, and say "Hello."

The wrong way would be to not say anything to the person of interest but instead to start silently following him or her and perhaps staring intently. This is bound to make the person being shadowed nervous. When the person turns around and looks upset, this is not rejection—it means the person being followed does not like it and does not want to engage in conversation because he or she does not know anything about the person following. This is a good example of the hidden curriculum.

We know that group activities, such as community service as mentioned in Chapter 7, can be a great way to form friendships and learn the hidden curriculum strategies by observing what others do. (I shared the story of how I met my first wife while doing community service in college at a nearby orphanage.) Engaging in sports, attending campus events, and joining special interest groups (such as an IT club) will provide the stepping-stones your son or daughter needs for going out socially to meet new friends and expand horizons. It is good "on the job" training for observing the instincts of others and gaining the critical, often not noticed (by the "Aspie") hidden curriculum knowledge.

Expressing emotion is often difficult for those of us on the autism spectrum. I actually learned about feeling loved, being loved, and giving love through my relationships with various pets during my childhood and adolescence. Animals teach children, young adults, and adults with learning differences to step outside of themselves and learn to care for others.

Learning to love through dogs

AT LEAST MY DOGS LOVE ME

—THE CHILDREN ALL GO ELSEWHERE

— THE GIRL FRIEND IS OUT TO FIND
HERSELF

BUT MY DOGS WILL KISS ME

AND RESPOND TO MY TOUCH

PEOPLE ARE HUMAN — THEY DO
WHAT THEY DO —

I'M A SURVIVOR

BUT I STILL GET BLUE

MY DOGS WON'T KISS ME WHEN I'M
CRYIN' —

THEY ARE AFRAID OF MY
EMOTION

GUESS I'LL JUST HAVE TO LOVE
MYSELF —

LIKE MY GOD DOES

3/7/07

Like many children with Asperger's Syndrome, I had better relationships with my dogs than with any other human being. My dogs slept in my bed and they were a source of affection and attachment for me. I became responsible for taking them out for walks and feeding them. Relating to animals was much easier than relating to people. My cherished pets became my security blanket. As I played with them, talked to them, and cared for them, I felt unconditionally loved.

My first dog's name was Max and he was a "boxer." He was a real smart dog and I spent hours teaching him tricks and lavishing attention on him. My sensory issues seemed to disappear when he kissed me all over my face. Those of us with Asperger's usually like dogs because they display the same emotional demeanor over and over again. For instance, I could always depend on Max to greet me enthusiastically the same way every single day. I liked that he was quiet and did not talk, and that I could do repetitive actions (such as petting him or roughhousing with him) repeatedly. Barring any allergies, dogs are a good way for your son or daughter to give and receive affection, learn about caring for others, and practice talking, communicating, and expressing emotion in a very safe environment.

The Director of our center in Melbourne, Florida, has a friend who brings a sweet little terrier named Clarence to the student lounge once a week. As the friend walks in the door with the dog, our students are often engaged in studying, or working one-on-one with a tutor or mentor. The room is quiet and each student is engaged in a special interest or homework and rarely looks up. Within seconds of the dog arriving, everyone is talking, petting the dog, engaging with others about the dog, how much he has grown, how funny he is, and so on. The students then continue talking about the dog to his owner and keep on chatting about the dog after he has left. A room full of immobile adolescents suddenly comes alive when nine pounds of fur walks in each week! Clarence is a great social motivator.

Sexual abuse prevention

Children on the autism spectrum are highly susceptible to sexual abuse because of their emotional isolation from others and their lack of social understanding. Children, adolescents, and young adults for the most part are often oblivious to social boundaries. This is why hidden curriculum instruction and being able to know the signs of abuse or profiles of abusers is so critical.

Many neurotypicals will sense danger, feel uncomfortable, or get an inner sense that something is not right. This ability needs teaching through raising awareness and imparting knowledge to those on the autism spectrum.

At CIP, we know that our young adults may not have experienced touch or intimacy with another person because they keep themselves isolated. As stated many times in this book, it is not uncommon for our students to spend all their time absorbed in their special interests. This isolation leads to emotional distance from parents, siblings, friends, relatives, and teachers. It also leaves them vulnerable when they do venture out on their own.

Parents need to tell their sons and daughters that most predators are trusted relatives or friends, and acquaint them with what good touch means and what inappropriate touch consists of. Talking to and imparting as much knowledge as you can about safety in relationships, and about normal and expected boundaries, to your son or daughter is vital.

In my case, I was abused at the age of five by a second cousin in our car while my mother was in the front seat driving and in our home when she was in another room cooking dinner. I was an isolated quiet child who did not like being touched, but I was manipulated by my cousin as he gained my trust while joining me in my special interest activity.

In our Relationship Development classes, we talk a lot about this and then give our students strategies and techniques for staying safe. We talk about power in relationships and how it is used and abused. In my situation, there was a lot of "implied violence" and "subtle intimidation" that I was unconscious of.

We will also refer any student whom we suspect or know has been abused (in the present or past) to a counselor who will then help him or her to heal, cope, and take appropriate action.

Knowledge is everything, and our students "get this." To know the difference between appropriate or inappropriate touch, without imparting fear or making them more phobic, is the focus of our unit on sexual abuse. For instance, we teach that there are different rules when you are 5 years old than when you are 25 years old and that these rules evolve as understanding evolves. We also let them know that, as a person changes and develops, his or her personal code of conduct or internal rules may change.

The hidden curriculum for our students is often learning to know and understand when it is appropriate to touch another person. At what age? Where? How much? How long? Neurotypicals seem to figure this out easily; those with Asperger's, autism, or learning differences need to be taught how to set limits and rules, and exactly what social boundaries "are." My difficulty with this persisted into adult years—that is, understanding the "unwritten" social boundaries both physically and verbally.

Jeremy's story and his lack of mastery in the hidden curriculum of friendship and dating illustrates what I am trying to say.

JEREMY

Jeremy was diagnosed with Asperger's Syndrome at an early age and was 19 years old when he enrolled in our Berkeley, California, Center. Although he desperately wanted to form relationships with young women, he had no real-life understanding or experience in approaching a member of the opposite sex, nor did he understand the hidden curriculum subtleties of flirting. He tended to be a loner. Although he was attracted to women, he did not attempt to initiate any kind of conversation or dialogue with them. In addition, if by chance a young woman initiated a conversation with him, he did not understand that he was supposed to respond or even how to respond.

Jeremy decided he liked and wanted to date an attractive young woman who was attending CIP. Even though the young woman made it very clear that she was not interested in him romantically, and was in fact dating another student, Jeremy continued to pursue her in an aggressive manner. He did not realize that this behavior was inappropriate.

Jeremy had an idea and thought that, if he could provide gifts and favors to young women, they would find him attractive and would want to enter into a relationship with him. While this approach may work under certain circumstances with some women, as usual Jeremy took his idea to "Aspie" extremes.

If a woman wanted a ride somewhere to buy shoes, or to the grocery store, or to the gym, Jeremy would drop everything in his life to accommodate her needs. This included missing college classes or work in order to do this. Jeremy soon began failing classes and losing jobs because he had no time for anything but driving his newly found and acquired "girl" friends wherever they wanted to go. He had no idea he was being used, and that the young women really were not interested in him (only his car), and he misread all the hidden curriculum social cues that were being presented to him.

Jeremy became obsessed with a young woman who exchanged simple social pleasantries with him on one occasion. Since Jeremy didn't have the social skills necessary to determine if the woman was interested in him in a romantic way or was just being polite and friendly, he decided, without asking for input or advice from anyone (or even thinking about using the famous donkey rule), that the woman was attracted to him. He began following her around the campus. He started showing up at her classes, even if he was not in that class. This behavior, very understandably, caused great concern for the young woman, and she firmly asked him to stop.

Jeremy continued to follow her wherever she went. She in turn began to feel like she was being stalked by him. In an effort to feel safe, the young woman asked campus security to intervene. Jeremy was approached by security, questioned, and told to stop his "stalker type" behavior at once. You can imagine how confused and humiliated Jeremy was. He truly did not understand that what he had done was inappropriate.

It took months of intervention via individual counseling, meetings with his advisor and social mentor, and attendance at his Relationship Development class and social thinking appointments before Jeremy could understand that the young woman felt threatened by his actions. He never got to the point where he completely understood why the woman felt threatened by his actions, but he could begin to understand that his behavior was inappropriate and had caused another person to feel uncomfortable and, at times, threatened. Staff worked with the Relationship Development class, and then, to reinforce it, with Jeremy individually, about the rules and laws of society that impart legal consequences on stalkers.

The relationship maze

My girlfriend wrote the following question for a "question and answer session" on a panel discussing "Relationships and Asperger's" at a conference in Long Island a few years ago. She wrote:

> I am in love with an amazing man who has Asperger's Syndrome. However, I often feel I am unable to connect with him on an intimate level that I feel is appropriate, but appears completely unimportant to him. I often feel I am on a different planet or wavelength. What ideas or suggestions do you have for me?

I was on the panel and knew it was her question as soon as they read it. After 16 months of living with me, and many, many heartfelt discussions about my Asperger's Syndrome, she still did not fully understand me. After 16 months of reading articles in magazines and many books, attending professional workshops, and being willing to learn all she could about Asperger's Syndrome, she still could not fully comprehend my differences.

I know that I am capable of being sensitive to others and, when I am in a relationship, I will often do wonderful or generous things for others. I try my best to live morally, to act with kindness and love, and my actions are genuine. At the same time, I can be oblivious to the needs of others around me. At times, I will follow an "internal script" that tells me to listen or to be present in a situation.

During these times, I will listen but I will be analyzing everything being said to me. I will then correct the person if I feel he or she is imparting knowledge that is wrong or not based in what I know to be the accurate "facts." If someone is using incorrect grammar, or states something that is illogical, I will focus on this instead of what he or she is saying. You can imagine how frustrating it would be for anyone who is trying to be in a deeper relationship with me.

When out socially I often do one of two things, stay aloof and isolated, or try to dominate the conversation and convince people of my intelligence or political correctness. In the end, this behavior and lack of my own mastery of the social nuances for building relationships get me nowhere. My inability to be with others in a reciprocal manner motivates me to work really hard in this area.

Through knowing, mastering, and practicing the techniques learned from the hidden curriculum work of Brenda Smith Myles and others, I have learned to initiate and give my time more freely. By working hard on the areas CIP's Relationship Development class focuses on, I have learned and continue working on and improving my reciprocal conversation skills. I have learned to read the facial expressions of others and I am more aware of when it is time to end a conversation or let someone else talk. Most importantly, I have slowly learned to accept the love of others even though I am imperfect.

I'd like to tell you about Glen—as in my story above, Glen had no role model or mentor during his formative years that could show him how to navigate dating, and no one to talk to or confide in. Glen felt comfortable coming to me and this is his story.

GLEN

Twenty-five years ago, before we talked about Asperger's as freely as we do now or talked about dating or even sex for that matter, one of my students, Glen, came to me and asked me about dating. He wanted to know how to ask someone out on a date and what he should do. Glen had an absentee father and his mom had emotional issues of her own and was unable to communicate effectively or "be there" for Glen. He was more or less "on his own."

Glen talked to me about not knowing how to ask someone out and he talked about how much he wanted to experience everything that his peers were doing, specifically "dating." Because of his upbringing (or lack thereof), he wanted someone to genuinely care for him and about him. Glen also wanted to experience intimacy and being loved.

Because of his learning differences, Glen was a 20-year-old with the emotional intelligence of a 13-year-old. Looking back on this situation, I realize now that, even though I was married and had several children of my own at the time, I was not too far ahead of him. He and I had a lot in common and I really wanted to try to help him.

We talked several times and I helped Glen make a plan that later became the basis for CIP's Relationship Development class. I asked him to start with saying "Hi" to someone he was interested in. Then he would ask her to have coffee, or to go to a movie, and then he would ask to see her again the following week. We wrote all this out in great detail even though it was just a few simple steps.

The document turned out to be many pages long. It contained a list of all the little things you do to get to know another person. It was (in reality) a guide to reciprocal conversation skills. I listed all the techniques for showing interest in what another person has to say, what response would be appropriate, then how to move on to another subject, and finally how to end a conversation.

All those many years ago, I was able to impart this knowledge to Glen and, all these many years later, I still work hard to implement these techniques myself. Mastering the hidden curriculum of friendship, dating, and all that this entails through CIP's relationship development coursework allows our students to further embrace the unique individuals that they are, and to be able do this with pride and confidence.

As stated in Chapter 1, self-knowledge and self-acceptance of a diagnosis sets the stage for mastering the techniques and skills necessary for your son or daughter's success in building relationships with others. And, once again, the phrase that appears from time to time in this book (and that is actually the title of the last chapter) is one I continue to impart to our students during this process: the genuine evokes the genuine—and when you are your true self and who you truly are, you will attract to you the right person to be in a relationship with.

Chapter 11

Learning Openness, Tolerance, and Diversity

Be Yourself... Everyone Else is Taken

May you recognize in your life the presence, power, and light of your soul and have respect for your individuality and difference.

SYNCRONICITY

UNDERSTANDING HOW YOU FEEL ...

SEEING YOUR EMOTIONS AND RELATING ...

ENJOYING LISTENING TO IT ALL ...

THE CREATIVITY ...

THE HONESTY ....

THE EMPATHY ...

THE EMOTION ....

WANTING TO RELATE MORE AND ON A DEEPER LEVEL

TO ABSORB ....

TO LEARN ...

TO SHARE ...

TO BE WITH ...

THE REMARKABLE INTELLIGENCE, VISION

AND INTUITION ...

A GIVING NATURE ...

AN OPEN SPIRIT ...

A LOVER OF LIFE ...

The optimist says the glass is half-full, the pessimist says the glass is half-empty, and the "Aspie" says the glass is made of silicon, melted, and then formed into a shape to hold liquids for humans to drink. It is usually clear, but can be colored by adding dye during the process.

As a parent (and especially a parent of a child on the autism spectrum), you know that you need to be prepared for "anything and everything!" I know from much experience of being the father of six children that parents cannot foresee or prevent the mistakes their children will make and at some point your son or daughter will need to stand on his or her own and learn from making mistakes. As much as you may want to, you cannot prevent your children's lives from unfolding in less than perfect ways.

As a child, I watched my parents cope with the suicides of two of my siblings, one of their parents, two of their uncles, one son-in-law, and two grandchildren. To this day, I cannot imagine all the pain, and all the hurt, they endured. Moreover, I know that, if this were to happen to one of my own children, it would be unbearable. I use and encourage all parents to create and impart pro-active strategies to help their children cope with day-to-day emotions as well as the deeper challenges and tragedies of life. This is vital for children, adolescents, and young adults on the autism spectrum. Creating emotional outlets through open dialogue, honesty, and learning from your own experiences (positive and negative) will foster positive feelings and well-being in your sons and daughters.

Michael John Carley says, "Love helps, purpose helps, and our attitudes toward our lives seem to play a far bigger role than the events in our lives themselves" (2008, p.228).

Pre-teaching and imparting knowledge are key even though there may be a gap in your son or daughter's ability to implement this information and training. It will give him or her the foundation for learning to make the most out of each challenging situation. At CIP, we continue what you have started. We help students learn from mistakes, move forward from them, and continue to feel and deal with the emotions around them. This ongoing reframing work helps our students revisit and talk about the emotions surrounding decisions, events, or incidents that are happening to them or have happened to them.

As discussed in Chapter 3, reframing allows your son or daughter to process his or her emotions, and to use this knowledge to look at events in a new light. Your son or daughter learns that the reframing process will be a tool and technique that he or she can use throughout his or her life.

Dale Carnegie (1960) said:

> Having courage does not depend on what is happening outside you. It depends entirely on what is happening *inside* you. Only thoughts can give you courage, and only thoughts can give you fear. So begin right now thinking thoughts of courage. (p.123)

As adults, we still look back at our childhood and young adulthood and process what we went through. We usually stop blaming our parents and others at some point and take responsibility for our own emotional well-being. We change the CDs in the CD player in our brain. We substitute new CDs that say positive mantras to us. We use our own form of cognitive behavior therapy on ourselves and we move forward. My friend Paul tells me that I need to "fire the writers" in my brain and start writing some new scripts.

Young adults on the autism spectrum do not have the wisdom of adults, or even the wisdom of those not on the spectrum who have the same chronological age as they do.

Our students tend to see only what is right in front of them and to take things extremely literally. They lack experience of "living through" the "ups and downs" that their neurotypical peers have had. Because of isolation and being generally more protected and sheltered by parents, children, adolescents, and young adults on the autism spectrum lack the perspective and understanding that "this too shall pass" and "a new dawn will come." I had a difficult time processing my grandmother's and siblings' suicides and, because of my inability to express emotion, I was like the "toxic sponge" I described in Chapter 3.

Perspective for those with learning differences is harder to achieve and occurs (on average) four to five years later than for their neurotypical counterparts. Many of our students do not settle into a "groove" or find their niche emotionally and socially until they are in their late 20s.

Acceptance and diversity

At CIP, we teach acceptance and foster diversity through classroom instruction using illustrative events and media. We know that our students can be judgmental, analytical, disapproving, and rigid in their thinking about other people. These are all traits that correlate with Asperger's, autism, and learning differences. This lack of tolerance toward others can be exacerbated by their own depression or lack of self-esteem. The combination of depression and traits characteristic of the autism spectrum often leads to a maelstrom during the teen and young adult years.

Our students sense that something is wrong with their thinking and they do not like it. They do not have the knowledge, acceptance, or tolerance to do something concrete about what they are feeling. Anger swells and outbursts occur. There are solutions, and things will get better. Only those who have lived with this situation understand the frustration and the need to try new things, accept things where they are at, and move on.

This formative period is the time for all young adults on the autism spectrum to recognize and embrace diversity. The more accepting they become of themselves, the more people's differences will become acceptable to them in a peaceful way. Self-acceptance and tolerance can release them from a lifetime of rigidity and pain.

Through CIP's social thinking process, we work to help our students understand and appreciate the differences in other people, and enjoy the wonderful and wide array of diversity that exists in the human race.

The analytical minds of those on the autism spectrum often mean our students are preoccupied with technical information and less available to make or maintain relationships with others. The

"Aspie" analytical brain gets in the way and often ties a young person into one single-minded way of seeing the world. At CIP, we want our young adults to become citizens of the world, fully able to navigate the world with openness and a constructive attitude.

As mentioned before, I love the saying "The roller coaster is better than the merry-go-round," and this applies here as well. Allowing your son or daughter to get on that roller coaster and not settle for the merry-go-round allows for looking at the world with wonder and awe. Helen Keller said, "Life is either an adventure or nothing at all."

Adolescence is an especially formative period in our students' lives and the time for them to recognize and embrace diversity. The more accepting our young adults become, the more people's differences will become acceptable to them *and* in a peaceful and respectful way.

Tolerance is nurtured through self-acceptance of one's self. Acceptance of diagnosis, then self, can release your son or daughter from a lifetime of rigidity and pain, and open up the world around him or her.

When attending college, your son or daughter will be living in a community where more people are students than are not. This will be the basis for making friends, sharing common interests, and noticing differences. There will be many opportunities to learn about the larger world. By taking the time to find out about the differences of others and then slowly start to embrace qualities that may be different or seem "foreign" in those around them, everyone grows. You can mentor this by setting examples and bringing diversity into your home.

Sometimes students with learning differences have anger toward others with more obvious disabilities. This is a defense mechanism. Students often point the finger at others to take the spotlight off themselves. They think that they can feel better about themselves if someone else appears worse off than they are. We know from experience that this is often just an indication of low self-esteem.

Our students are often living with a dichotomy. They might be in a class where the discussion turns to religion. They might be surprised to find that there are students who practice different religions from their own.

Through interactions, social activities, and listening to stories and beliefs, young adults learn to start acknowledging and accepting the views of others. They also realize with time, and experience in these interactions, that this does not diminish their own values or beliefs.

CIP's Berkshire Center had a male student from Saudi Arabia attending our program at the same time as a female student from Israel. They became best of friends. When I talked to the male student, he claimed that he hated Israel and Jewish people. He refused to attend a convocation we had using a local church because there was a crucifix displayed on the wall. The girl from Israel also claimed that she did not want anything to do with Muslims, and did not want to alter her views. While they both held these intolerant and set-in-stone views, they only saw each other as "friends" and never talked religion or politics.

My friend Nick Dubin writes in his book about AS and anxiety that:

> A negative core belief is a giant cognitive distortion that has been accepted as fact, without any questioning or critical thinking surrounding it. It's what I like to call a "distortion dogma." Secondary appraisal loses its purpose once these negative core beliefs solidify. The core beliefs serve as roadblocks barring the way for thoughtful alternatives. Once a person forms negative core beliefs, it is not likely he or she will consider alternative measures. Do you see how narrow and dangerous this kind of thinking can become without intervention? (2009, p.83)

My own experiences that I detail below are reflected in Nick's statement.

MICHAEL'S QUEST—DO I WANT TO BE RIGHT OR DO I WANT TO BE HAPPY?

As a young adult, I was frustrated in my dealings with others. I could not agree with my peers on many issues, but at the same time I desperately wanted to be friends with them. I felt isolated and alone and clung to my beliefs that, in reality, separated me from others. I would outwardly respect others in public, but secretly not accept them as having a "valid existence" in private. If they did not believe in my religion or my way of being in the world, I became even more intolerant.

As an adult, I had to learn (sometimes the hard way by making obvious faux pas) to suspend my judgments of others. I learned, after my diagnosis, to listen to others and ask them questions about who they were, where they came from, and what was important to them. I came across this saying while practicing my newfound diversity: "Do you want to be right or do you want to be happy?" These words helped me break through the cognitive rigidity that seemed to always be engulfing my brain. It was a spiritual solution for me also. I logically realized that a "loving God" would not send two to three billion Muslims, Buddhists, Jews, and Protestants to Hell; therefore, they must be acceptable for me to love also.

I learned that I do not have to agree with everyone and they do not have to agree with me. I can still be friends with people of all different religions and political, racial, and national origins, and still be me. Sort of like our Saudi student and our Israeli student were able to do.

This is a student's time to recognize and embrace diversity. Learning about the differences of others becomes acceptable and at times a bridge to true understanding. This acceptance and tolerance is called "internal growth." At CIP, learning tolerance and being open to others with differences sets the scene for a lifetime practice of "the genuine evoking the genuine."

Person-centered planning

This is every CIP student's *Declaration of Independence*. They get to declare their individual hopes, dreams, and ambitions. They then sketch them out as a "road map for the future." Unlike high school and grade school where a student's family, teachers, administrators, and professionals dictated his or her "education plan" through an Individualized Educational Plan (IEP) and the student just sat there and listened, person-centered planning allows each young adult to express what he or she wants, needs, or would like.

The person-centered plan is then presented to the student's family and staff in a PowerPoint format that explains all the things that are important to the individual. The PowerPoint presentation might include music, photographs and important mementos, videos of people, places and things the person likes, art, pets, places, and even a job or activities that brought happiness or joy.

Our students come to embrace this process and we know from experience that many continue this person-centered planning activity throughout key and important periods in their lives.

In each section of the person-centered plan, students clearly write out individual thoughts in the following areas:

1. Character: what qualities do they want to develop in themselves?

2. Values: what are the important values that guide their lives?

3. Support: what people, experiences, or institutions give direction to their lives?

4. Strengths: what talents and abilities do they have?

5. Motivators: what motivators do they use to motivate themselves?

6. Dreams: what are the three or four main dreams they want to accomplish?

Students are then encouraged to write a "personal mission statement" that embraces a core understanding of what "makes them tick." This is an example written by a student named Sean from Seattle:

Sean

I have a very strong desire to succeed at anything that I try and am very competitive. I am a person who fears failure and is enormously motivated by economic security and wealth. I plan to make a lot of money. I am motivated by good grades.

I will bring to any situation my very strong work ethic and sense of ethics. I plan to use my strong leadership skills and strong problem-solving skills. I have a firm belief in maintaining good physical and mental health. This includes maintaining good relationships with my family and my peers. When with them, I want to work well, enjoy their company, and communicate my feelings without hiding anything. I want to stay in good physical health, too, without hurting my body in any way, be it through injury, alcohol, or drugs. I recently found out by injuring my arm how important sports are to me to maintain my emotional balance and focus. I persevere and want to work hard, however.

In summary, my personal mission is to maintain my mental and physical health through exercise and meditation and playing the sports that I enjoy. I have learned to calm myself down and to decrease my tendency to anger quickly with others. I will continue to practice meditation. I envision an open, honest, and happy relationship with both of my parents.

In my career, I will utilize my passion for sports and my interest in psychology while being successful, independent, and calm. I will control my anger at work and have time to be with my family. I will stay relaxed through exercise and meditation. By working independently and having control over my schedule, I will be able to stay calm and centered through good self-care.

Not all students have the insight that Sean developed to be able to write on this level of understanding about themselves. At CIP, all students receive coaching to help the process by clarifying some of the core issues that are important to each of them.

Julie, one of our students from Maine, wrote the following.

Julie

I am someone who has always liked acting and the arts. I love helping people and I love to laugh and to feel part of a group. Every summer I have been in plays and special art projects. For the longest time I have wanted to help children feel better about themselves. I know what it is like to feel different and lonely. Someday I would like to be a therapist, and use the creative arts to help kids to feel more open about their feelings, freer, and more spontaneous. I know how alive and well I feel when I act and create artistic collages.

It is my life's dream to use the creative arts, including drama and painting, as a therapeutic tool. I would love to be affiliated someday with a hospital that treats seriously ill children with this type of therapy. I have an altruistic love for helping people and like to connect people with others. I want to help children to be well and happy with themselves.

I am also someone who has a big need to be my own person. I have lots of unique ideas and my own personal style. I enjoy working in my own way, and want to have my separate niche and place where I can excel. I like enough creative space for expressing my uniqueness. I like the time to adjust to change and want to work with people I like and trust. I need complete directions to get my work done and I do not like conflict and confrontation. I like a lot of predictability in my environment. I am definitely someone who wants a small college with small classes and a very friendly campus. I like developing good relationships with my teachers. It is important to me to be part of a team so that I do not feel like I am alone when I help children. I would like to work part-time in the beginning, to not feel too overwhelmed, and to make sure that I am not too stressed out. My dream is to have a family of my own someday and a career that allows for part-time hours when I have my own children.

My most important goal is to take good care of my mental and physical health and to not resort to self-destructive behaviors again. I want to stay healthy and relaxed, and to continue to enjoy drama and the arts.

Sean and Julie were able to communicate quite well what they wanted through their personal mission statements.

Through mission statements, students draft their goals for the future, starting with long-term goals and moving to short-term or immediate needs and wants. Goals are easier to achieve when they are specific and detailed, and written down in the present tense. At CIP, we set clear time limits for planning and goal-setting so that we can help students track and begin to achieve them. It is important for our students, too, to set time limits on accomplishing goals, and these are written down and clarified as well.

Most goals are accomplished in partnership with others, and our students soon learn that almost everything we do in life is in relationship with others. As part of the process, some of the students viewed episodes of some of the *Survivor* shows that are on television. These shows introduced and reinforced the concepts of creating alliances with others, and used input and advice from others to solve problems and dilemmas (an expansion, more or less, of the donkey rule).

Many students on the autism spectrum have a built-in default to "go it alone," which works against them in the adult world. They need to be taught and then learn to build partnerships and alliances for accomplishing the goals expressed in their mission statements.

We ask our students to write down what they think would be the best approach for our staff to work with them during their time in the program sessions. Sometimes, we have to "tease it out of them" and show them how to express what they are trying to say.

A modification of this process can also be used for self-disclosure in college or at work—for example, to a professor or with an employer at a job site. Alan, one of our students from Ohio, wrote a very clear statement that helped him at CIP, in college, and when working at his part-time job:

Alan

I am forward-looking, aggressive, and competitive. My vision for obtaining results is one of my positive strengths. I am often frustrated when working with others who do not share the same sense of urgency. I can be blunt and critical of people who do not meet my standards. I may be reluctant to delegate certain tasks and slow to trust others to meet my own high standards.

I am extremely results-oriented and have a sense of urgency to complete projects quickly. I have high ego strengths and I am a self-starter who likes new projects and am most comfortable being highly involved with a wide scope of activities. I am sensitive to errors and mistakes. I do not get emotionally involved in decision-making. I sometimes require assistance in bringing major projects to completion. I am logical, incisive, and critical of my problem-solving activities.

I tend to communicate in a cool and direct manner. I will want you to communicate with me in a clear, precise, and brief conversation. I will need regular performance appraisals from you to keep me on task and have parameters and timelines put into writing. I will struggle somewhat to be objective and listen to any constructive criticism. I will easily grasp the big picture as well as the small pieces of the puzzle and be persistent in completing the necessary steps of the college planning process, including being attentive to detail.

When communicating with me, know that I look for straight talk supported by facts, tangible evidence, and information presented in a logical order. Help me to feel more in control of my own destiny by allowing me an environment where I can ask specific questions. I do best when there is limited socializing and more facts and data presented for making decisions. I have a strong desire to lead, direct, and control my own destiny and the destiny of others. If others try to impose their way of living or thinking on me, I will become frustrated.

Who says students can't tell you what their needs are!
Brianna, a student from Delaware, wrote the following.

Brianna

I am someone who requires many reasons to make choices and changes. I need to understand the full benefits of making a change. It is important to me that others be warm and personal in their communications with me.

Once I make a decision, it becomes very difficult for me to change my mind. While I am flexible enough to fit into any environment, I tend to fight for my beliefs or those things I feel passionate about. Once I have arrived at a decision, I can be tough-minded and unbending. I like to collect a great deal of data before making any important decision. I am very persistent in meeting my goals.

Know that I tend to conceal any grievances or opinions that may differ with yours. I will not easily state my feelings. Reaching a trust level with you may take more time than with other students, although I will always be cordial and friendly.

I have much personal strength. I am highly service-oriented, good at reconciling factions and am calming, and add stability. I can turn confrontation into positives and am quite people-oriented. I like to work for a leader and a cause and am highly adaptable and flexible.

I long for a warm and friendly environment and a feeling of belonging. I need to know I am important to my team.

You may have seen the attributes, strengths, traits, and dreams of your own son or daughter in the examples listed here. Many professionals claim that insight-centered therapy is unavailable to people on the autism spectrum—that they cannot take advantage of this because of their myopic sense of themselves and the world around them. We have found the person-centered planning process supports students in stating their vision for themselves and in identifying the personal strategies that they will need to develop to reach their goals. It expands their thinking in many ways. We often let the students sit with some popcorn and refreshments and watch each other's person-centered-planning PowerPoint presentations. This is a revelation for many of our students. Seeing and hearing someone else's vision and goals with personal music and pictures and special interests displayed throughout is often as life-changing for the viewer as it is for the presenter.

When students see 10 or 12 of their peers' visions for themselves expressed so uniquely, they get contrasts for comparison and are able to analyze their own situations a little more clearly.

Person-centered planning leads to young adults becoming "change-makers" and, moreover, learning to be whom they dream of being and want to be. It gives a blueprint for taking on their own unique world and bringing forth their own unique talents, gifts, hopes, and dreams to others.

Elaine Hall writes in her book:

> Now I see the moon. I have come to understand autism as a gift that can uplift everyone it affects, for autism teaches us the highest values: to accept and cherish others for who they are, to revere rather than dread the differences between us, to acknowledge that there is no right or wrong way—that there is only your way and my way and that both are valid. (Hall with Kaye 2010, p.273)

Chapter 12

Moving Forward

The Genuine Evokes the Genuine

Like flowers that grow out of volcanic rock, we blossom despite our past eruptions, even in the most sparse conditions.

Becoming a "change master"

As we approach working with our students, we ask them to be willing "to grow." This is more palatable than asking them "to change." It has been our experience that young adults are stuck in the process of making changes and this sometimes surfaces as anxiety or procrastination. In AA, they say, "Move a muscle, change a thought." This quote certainly has credence. Getting into *action*, any action, whether this is a plan, thinking creatively, or trying something new, is better than doing nothing at all.

I often tell our students that we simply do not learn without some unease and, at times, conflict. If there is no wind in the sail, you are not going anywhere, so I encourage them to set sail, in a dinghy if need be; the sailboat can come later.

On a recent trip to Athens, my flight took me from Hartford to Dallas. I would then take a flight from Dallas to Madrid and then one to Athens. When I got to the airport, the flight to Madrid from Dallas was showing a half-hour delay. I knew that my flight from Madrid was with a different carrier and that I had to get my bags, then recheck in at a different terminal upon arrival. At this point, I knew that I had four hours between flights, so I felt confident that I had enough time to get to my new airline in Madrid. I decided that I did not need to worry or think about this, because it seemed under control.

Back in Dallas the flight delay was extended to 45 minutes because of maintenance problems with the plane, and then to an hour and finally to an hour and a half. I started to get somewhat anxious and found myself constantly calculating the time difference with the delay and then using that to figure out the remaining time I would have left to make the other flight. The plane was eventually towed into the gate and we were ready to board. No sooner did this happen when it was announced that they needed to run the engines for a while to be ready. I then waited another 20 minutes. Finally, they started to load the plane at (what I was anxiously thinking was) a "snail's pace." When everyone was seated, the flight crew announced they had to run the engines, turn them off, and then have the maintenance department verify that the original problem was fixed. This took another half hour. As the plane taxied (this took forever) to the take-off runway, I was convinced we had driven halfway to Madrid.

I recalculated that I now had about an hour between flights to get to the other airline, check bags, and board the other flight. Then I realized I had to go through customs, get my luggage and proceed to another terminal, check in, go through security, and get to the new airline's gate. I made the correct assumption that this would not be possible unless the other plane to Athens was late in taking off. Moreover, I began to relax (something the "old" Michael would not have been able to do).

When we approached Madrid, the pilot announced that we were being put in a delay pattern and would land in about 15 or 20 minutes. Having accepted the fact earlier that I would miss my flight to Athens, I figured I would just rebook on a later flight in the afternoon or early evening and that it would not be a problem.

Upon arrival in Madrid, I went through all the customs, baggage, etc., took the bus to the next terminal, and went to the airline booth for Aegean Airlines only to find that it was closed. The person in the next booth said that Aegean only ran one flight to Athens each day and that the next flight would be at the same time the following day. I decided to get back on the bus, return to the terminal where my flight had come in, and see if American Airlines could help me. Of course they could, but they would charge me an additional $1600. I called another airline (Lufthansa) and was told the same thing—they could help me, but it would cost about the same amount of money.

Surprisingly and despite having little sleep throughout this whole process, I remained calm. I knew that one way or the other the situation would work out. Putting all my internal and external calming techniques into place, I was able to come up with another idea and plan. I decided to call Aegean Airlines in Athens. After stating my case, Aegean gave me credit for the flight and booked me out on the first flight for the next day. Buoyed by my luck in telephoning Greece directly, I then contacted the hotel in Athens to tell them I would not be arriving. They kindly did not charge me for the missed evening in their hotel. On a roll now, I called the taxi service and changed the pick-up to the next day; finally (being my own superior customer service agent by this point), I went up to the hotel counter and booked a room in central Madrid.

Within a half hour, I was in my Madrid hotel room, showered, and about to have a nice meal at a sidewalk café. I spent the evening at the Prado Museum looking at the El Greco exhibits, and walking through the gardens of the Arboretum. I stopped to listen to some music at the festival Isadora and did some window-shopping in the warm evening breeze. I then returned to my room and painted a picture from the balcony.

I realized how quickly my learned and much practiced cognitive flexibility skills came into play. "I can be spontaneous if I plan on it." I was able to make a wonderful day out of a nerve-wracking and distressing situation. In addition, I knew where this newfound ability had come from—from gleaning knowledge about my Asperger's, practicing techniques to deal with my personal stressors, and then analyzing the changes in my behavior that I needed to make from within.

I was my own "change master." I had changed a negative thinking pattern to an optimistic and explorative one and then to a positive outlook, and I was able to cope. From many, many years of experience traveling and from having to deal with similar situations, I knew what did not work for me and I consciously made myself physically and mentally curb my anxiety.

Going back to the self-care basics, I need to function and live with my Asperger's Syndrome and so I made sure that I had some sleep medicine to take on the plane. I then used the techniques I described earlier in the book by putting my sensory travel diet into effect. I salvaged a few hours of precious sleep. I ate good foods (I had pre-ordered vegetarian meals ahead of time). I also ate the fruit and snacks that I had packed in my carry-on bag. I got up and stretched out for a half hour and I reminded myself throughout the process that "everything was for good purpose" and that problems often present opportunities. I convinced myself to remain calm and to just "go with the flow." When I ran into frustration after landing, I wanted to pick a fight and be grouchy but I made myself be nice to all the people I dealt with at each airline. Moreover, I thanked them for their help.

This was not the "Michael Meltdown" guy *of the past*. The one no one (not even me) wanted to be around. The Michael who exuded anxiety, fear, and anger. Instead, I took on the challenge, controlled my actions, and demonstrated commitment to the process by staying calm and in control. The words of William James came right into play—"If we want to change our lives we need to:

- start immediately
- do it flamboyantly
- make no exceptions or excuses."

I had every reason to blame the airlines and to be angry and miserable. Instead, I had a wonderful evening in Madrid filled with art, music, and food.

This outcome is the *culmination of the last eight years of working to understand, accept, and learn to live with my Asperger's Syndrome*. This is the example I set for our students. I am living proof that I practice what all CIP centers preach and teach. Our students can change their lives through action and being willing to grow. At CIP, we show our young adults through examples and experiences that the confusion and doubt they suffer from is avoidable. That fear and anxiety are optional. I say to them, "Have a great day, unless you decide otherwise not to." Slam-dunk!

Helping young adults become change masters

Thanks to my newfound understanding and knowledge from applying CIP's curriculum to myself, I have been able to develop the needed "social radar" that allows me to navigate the "higher order" areas of the adult world knowing that "All questions that lead to obtaining answers are intelligent." I am no longer afraid to speak up and ask questions, obtain information, and then to form partnerships with others or to try new things. Most of all I have learned to accept the opinions and ideas of others as not only legitimate but enriching to my life. This is a life worth living. This is what everyone involved at CIP strives to impart to our students: your sons and daughters.

Recently, I attended the end of the year convocation at the Berkshire Center in Lee, Massachusetts. At the end of the ceremony, five students who were moving on to four-year colleges or to live independently spoke.

I got emotional as I heard them all, in turn and in their own words, say that they had learned that they could motivate themselves and "know who they are." One said, "I don't know what I am going to do when I leave home, but I know how to do it!"

This is a poem I wrote right after college when I was full of idealism and desperately trying to get my actions to line up with my thoughts. I was trying so hard to create a life for myself, and discovered that I could express my feelings and learn to love others through my words, my art, and my actions.

Creating Thought Dreams in the Realm of Reality

Sometimes I have
to stand back
and say
"Was I really like that?"

It seems like just last
year that I was playing
schoolboy games
with life and
with God...

I never really related
to the thought–action
connection of my beliefs
Pockets of bitterness, hatred,
jealousy, and scorn existed
in me—as I hid in
the outward shell of my beliefs

Many soft breezes have
folded around me since then...

I have learned
from young children
what my political science professor
couldn't teach me

I have learned
Through old ladies' eyes
that which I was
Blind to...

Feelings—understanding—compassion—
How could I have let these slip
from my mind?

Now I have hope and can love...

Looking ahead—a legacy to those on the autism spectrum

As I stated in the introduction to the book, many post-secondary programs like mine exist. As CIP continues to grow nationally and internationally, I continue to look for cost-effective ways to provide our services to as many young adults as possible. To aid in offsetting direct costs to parents and families, I established the 501 (c) 3 not-for-profit foundation, the Student Educational Development Fund (SEDF), in 2006. This foundation will be my focus and my legacy to my students and their families as I move into the retirement phase of my life.

The mission of the foundation is the following:

• To provide financial support for the college educational and career needs in the form of scholarships for individuals with Asperger's Syndrome, non-verbal learning disabilities, high-functioning autism, attention deficit disorder, dyslexia, and other learning differences to attend post-secondary educational programming.

- To support the professional development of CIP staff responsible for providing the educational and support services required by the students we serve. To educate clinicians, professionals, and parents by providing educational seminars and conferences in the latest cutting-edge research in this field featuring the world's experts. In 2010, SEDF conducted six nationwide seminars that imparted knowledge to several hundred attendees. All proceeds from these conferences went to the SEDF Scholarship Fund.

- To support, encourage, and develop the visual and performing arts through studio instruction, workshops, and mentoring of students with local and regional artists in a studio, gallery, and performance space setting. In July 2011, the Spectrum Playhouse, Joyous Studios, Good Purpose Gallery, and the Starving Artist Café opened as a "pilot" at our Berkshire Center in Lee, Massachusetts. I hope to replicate this pilot at all CIP centers in the future. Proceeds from the pilot and future ventures will also benefit the SEDF Scholarship Fund.

*Please note that *all* royalties from the sale of this book are being donated to SEDF.

My plan going forward

My retirement plan is to work on behalf of the foundation. In many ways I have been one of the biggest recipients of CIP's work, especially since my diagnosis. By fulfilling SEDF's mission through strengthened outreach efforts, fundraising, and awareness, I complete the cycle of what I set out to do over 28 years ago— making it a reality for *as many young adults as possible* to learn about themselves so that they can go forward with confidence and pride into a world that is just learning *who they are, how they think, and all about the worth and goodness that they bring to those who get to know them.*

How to choose a program for your son or daughter

I am often asked to give advice about what to look for in considering or choosing a program to meet the needs of young adults on the autism spectrum. This is the information that CIP provides to parents, families, and care-givers who are investigating programs to meet the needs of adolescents and young adults who have been diagnosed with Asperger's Syndrome, autism, or learning differences.

General questions

- What kind of program would provide the best opportunity for academic success?

- What is the general location of the program (e.g., city, rural)?

- What is the program's mission and overall goals?

- How long has the program existed?

- What is the ratio of students to employees?

- What credentials do the employees have?

- What is the average length of stay?

- Is there an orientation process?

- Is there assistance for improving a student's social competencies?

- How is the student assessed in the different areas of the program (i.e., executive functioning, vocational, academic, clinical, sensory, residential, financial)?

- Are progress reports sent during the year? How many?

- Does the program provide meetings with relevant staff to discuss a student's progress? How often?

- Does the program have an active Student Senate participating in developing leadership, community service, and recreational outlets?

- Does the program offer a Parent Weekend with optional parent workshops?

- What happens during the summer months?

- Do students learn public transportation?

- Is there an Awards Convocation at the end of the year?

- What do students do once they leave the program?

- What are the additional costs above the tuition?

Academic support questions

- Does the program have liaison with colleges and universities?

- Is tutoring available? What kind? How often?

- Does the program offer study groups or supervised study halls?

- Is there a specific Asperger's/non-verbal curriculum, separate from the main curriculum?

- Does the program offer specific classes in executive functioning and theory of mind?

Social support questions

- Does the program offer social thinking groups?

- Are there Master's or Doctoral social mentors to work with the students?

- Is there a process and curriculum for social mentoring?

Advising support questions

- Will the student have an advisor that he or she meets with once or twice a week?

- Does the advisor keep regular contact with parents? What information is discussed?

- Does the advisor assist the student with a personal budget and banking?

- Does the advisor assist the student with a self-assessment and setting a weekly goal?

- How will the advisor assist the student in developing a person-centered plan or short- and long-term goals?

Independent living support questions

- What is the ratio of residential staff to students?

- Are live-in staff available for emergencies throughout the night? How many?

- Does the program provide individualized cooking instruction?

- Is there a menu-planning and shopping process?

- Is there training in cleaning, laundry, and maintaining the apartment?

- Do the residential staff work with implementing executive functioning checklists and assist the student in learning personal organizational skills?

- How are problems between roommates solved?

- Are roommates matched by similar interests and characteristics?

- Does the residential program offer a life skills class?

- Does the program provide driver's education?

Recreational support questions

- Will the student have a personal fitness plan?

- Does the program offer a fitness facility for students to attend?

- Is attendance mandatory? Supervised? Instructed? How are attendance problems handled?

- Does the program offer a variety of weekend and evening activities for students to attend? What about wellness classes such as art, dance, yoga, etc.?

- Are students required to attend a certain number of activities?

- Does the program offer a supervised travel program during spring breaks?

Sensory/wellness questions

- Does the program provide a sensory assessment?

- Does the program provide an occupational therapist to analyze this information and create a sensory diet for the student?

- Do the residential staff work in conjunction with the occupational therapist implementing sensory diets and a sensory profile?

- Is there a sensory integration class offered as part of the curriculum?

- Do students have a nutritional assessment with recommendations provided?

- What does the program do to reinforce wellness and good nutrition with the students?

Career development questions

- Does the program have a career coordinator who does assessments with the student?

- Is there a taught career class?

- Is community service required?

- How about assistance with students' finding and keeping internship positions?

- Does the program assist students in finding employment?

- Is career counseling provided?

- Are internship support groups provided?

Clinical/medication questions

- Does the program offer individual therapy on site? Is this part of the tuition?

- What type of therapy is used?

- What are the clinician's qualifications?

- Is there liaison with the student's psychiatrist?

- Is a medication coordinator available to assist students with setting up and ordering medications?

- Does the program provide access to any supplementary services (neurotherapy, hyperbaric therapy, etc.)?

- How does the program handle outside services (personal trainers, etc.)?

These are all important topics to cover when looking into a pre-college, college, transitional, or independent living program for your student with Asperger's, autism, or learning differences.

Epilogue

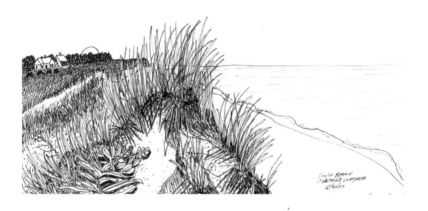

Wow! What a journey this continues to be for me. There seems to be no ending point to what we (as educators) are learning in terms of what young adults on the autism spectrum need and need to know. There is even more excitement in learning how to impart this knowledge in new and better ways. Each time I think I have discovered all there is to know about assisting young people on the spectrum, a new perspective or approach is presented.

CIP continues to grow and blossom, as does my understanding of what is required and how to achieve it. There is a tremendous need for more outreach to parents and for more programs to open in order to accommodate the growing population of young adults on the autism spectrum. There is an even greater need for these services to be affordable and available to all who require them.

As stated in my "retirement plan," the dream of embracing the talents that many of our students possess is coming true. The Berkshire Visual and Performing Arts Center (BVPAC) in Lee, Massachusetts, has indeed become a reality. The Spectrum Playhouse and the Good Purpose Art Gallery opened in July 2011 to showcase the art and performing arts talents of our students. Joyous Studios will offer instruction, mentoring, and creative development in a variety of media including photography, painting, and ceramics. Our National Art Contest is in full swing and hopes to expand internationally. Our Computer Graphics and Gaming Classrooms at each center have expanded as well. *Let there be no talent that is wasted!*

As I begin to shift from my current role at CIP into working on raising resources for the SEDF Scholarship Fund and advancing the foundation's mission, more students and families will be able to take advantage of the services my centers offer. This work (there really is no such thing as retirement) will help me achieve my lifelong dream and heartfelt prayer of leaving a legacy of hope and contribution for the next generation of young adults on the autism spectrum.

With love, light, hope, and joy,
Michael P. McManmon

McManmon family, 1952: I am the little boy
at the bottom left not making any eye contact

References

Bane Woodacre, M.E. and Bane, S. (2006) *I'll Miss You Too: What Will Change, What Will Not and How We'll Stay Connected*. Naperville, IL: Sourcebooks.

Bellini, S. (2006) *Building Social Relationships: A Systematic Approach to Teaching Social Interaction Skills to Children and Adolescents with Autism Spectrum Disorders and Other Social Difficulties*. Overland Park, KS: AAPC Publishing.

Bieber, J. (Producer) (1994) *Learning Disabilities and Social Skills with Richard Lavoie: Last One Picked... First One Picked On*. Washington, DC: Public Broadcasting Service.

Carley, M.J. (2008) *Asperger's from the Inside Out*. New York: Penguin.

Carnegie, D. (1960) *The Dale Carnegie Course in Effective Speaking and Human Relations*. Hauppauge, NY: Dale Carnegie and Associates.

Dubin, N. (2009) *Asperger's Syndrome and Anxiety*. London: Jessica Kingsley Publishers.

Edmonds, G. and Worton, D. (2005) *The Asperger Love Guide: A Practical Guide for Adults with Asperger's Syndrome to Seeking, Establishing and Maintaining Successful Relationships*. London: Lucky Duck Books.

Grandin, T. (1995) *Thinking in Pictures and Other Reports from My Life with Autism*. New York: Doubleday.

Hall, E. with Kaye, E. (2010) *Now I See the Moon*. New York: HarperCollins Publishers.

Johnson, M. (2005) *Managing with Asperger Syndrome: A Practical Guide for White Collar Professionals*. London: Jessica Kingsley Publishers.

Klin, A. (2010) Talk given at conference of the Asperger's Association of New England. Marlborough, MA, May 2010.

Rubinstien, M.B. (2005) *Raising NLD Superstars: What Families with Nonverbal Learning Disabilities Need to Know About Nurturing Confident, Competent Kids*. London: Jessica Kingsley Publishers.

Shore, S. (2003) *Beyond the Wall: Personal Experiences with Autism and Asperger Syndrome*. Overland Park, KS: AAPC Publishing.

Shore, S. (2010) *Understanding Asperger's Syndrome: Self-Advocacy and Self-Disclosure*. Conference presentation, January 12, Cranwell Resort, Lenox, MA.

Silverman, S.M. and Weinfeld, R. (2007) *School Success for Kids with Asperger's Syndrome*. Austin, TX: Prufrock Press.

Simmons, K.L. and Davis, B. (2010) *Autism Tomorrow: The Complete Guide to Help Your Child Thrive in the Real World*. Seattle, WA: SExceptional Resources.

Smith Myles, B., Trautman, M.L. and Schelvan, R.L. (2004) T*he Hidden Curriculum: Practical Solutions for Understanding Unstated Rules in Social Situations*. Overland Park, KS: AAPC Publishing.

Tammet, D. (2006) *Born on a Blue Day: Inside the Extraordinary Mind of an Autistic Savant*. New York: Free Press.

Tinsley, M. and Hendrickx, S. (2008) *Asperger Syndrome and Alcohol: Drinking to Cope*. London: Jessica Kingsley Publishers.

Zaks, Z. (2006) *Life and Love: Positive Strategies for Autistic Adults*. Overland Park, KS: AAPC Publishing.

Index